PROPERTY

The Conflict with Government's Monopoly on Force

Written by

Tim L. Smith, MPhil

Tim L. Smith

TLS - Independent Publishing

November 2017

Library of Congress Cataloging-in-Publication

ISBN - 13: 978-1979035101

ISBN - 10: 1979035105

Printed in the United States of America

For Jasmine and Avah

"The reason why men enter into society is the preservation of their property."

- John Locke

"The State lives by its very existence on the two-fold and pervasive employment of aggressive violence against the very liberty and property of individuals that it is supposed to be defending."

- Murray Rothbard

Content

"A right to property is founded in our natural wants, in the means with which we are endowed to satisfy these wants, and the right to what we acquire by those means without violating the similar rights of other sensible beings."

- Thomas Jefferson

When the responsibility that comes with freedom is not a part of the paradigm within public education, or society in general, children grow up to become adults that hold no affinity to their own personal liberty, or to property rights. Property rights are designed to secure property ownership. No longer do Americans truly own their property, or hold absolute control of their property. This is evident, in part, by the fact that people can no longer remain anonymous by choice, nor can people earn an honest living absent the government's forced, financial micromanagement of their right to earn a living, because money is property, and especially by the fact that no American can purchase real property absent the intrusion of government bureaucracy. Guns, money, assets, cars, homes, land, books, clothes, computers, cell phones, documents, art, etc, are all property and our rights ultimately derive from our property,[1] beginning with self-ownership. When you no longer truly own property, you no longer truly have rights. "For not only are there no human rights which are not also property rights, but the former rights [speech, defense, privacy] lose their absoluteness and clarity and become fuzzy and vulnerable when property rights are not used as the standard."[2] Instead of absolute property rights, you now have *legal privileges* and *legal possession*. In essence, we now have a government that takes our absolute property rights from us to protect us from people who might take our property from us. This is how government thinks. Property rights have been silently encroached upon by an invasive, neo-progressive philosophy, whereby, in part, one must *register* their valued property, by coercion, thus surrendering principle ownership and the rights attached to that property, to the state. This *legal plundering* then takes for granted that law enforcement will be there to impose the plundering. To register something or someone, has a very diversified history. Generally, to register something or someone means to record it, and/or make whatever is being registered a part of something else, to verify ownership or legal possession. However, *compulsory registration* has become a "legal" means for the state to acquire *jurisdiction* over either a person or their property. Jurisdiction is defined in Black's Law Dictionary, 8th Edition, as "A government's general power to exercise authority over all persons and things within its territory." Think about how much you register something with the government.

The cultivation of existing under a monarchy, made up of royalty, noblemen and commoners, unfortunately made its way into America's founding, minimally at first. The founders did not create the American system of government in a vacuum. Prior legal conditionings like *tort liability,* and the *law of contract,* for example, as it relates to property, were some of the foundations of American policy within the colonies. Why? The 18th century was a time when literally most people were uneducated and could not even read, but merely existed as farmers and of those simply trying to survive through servitude to land owners, and the like. Only the wealthy and educated owned land and participated in government. Thus, the *equal opportunity* for all people to own property was something that had to come about over time and the founders did establish a system, whereby, *absolute* property ownership of the *necessarily basic* would become the potential security against poverty and government intrusion for all Americans. Moreover, because property ownership was essential to securing liberty as a fundamental and natural right, Jefferson and

Washington, for example, pushed for public education. Education and being able to read was absolutely key to purchasing, owning and defending all natural rights, including property rights, as well as for participating in being self-governed. Otherwise, a person's purchasing power, income, and property rights would be greatly demoralized, not only by those wealthy businessmen in the new free market, but by government officials also. In addition, this is one reason why *pure* democracy was not instituted, but rather a *republic* was the initial form of government, because, most people simply did not posses the intellectual capacity to participate in government, yet. The Rule of Law would secure the restrictions upon those in government who wanted to exploit the ignorant and poor. Over time, public education has allowed most people to become somewhat educated. And, this sound progression in education has allowed for most people to "own" property. Unfortunately, however, this sound progression towards property ownership in early America has now digressed from a natural right then, into a legal privilege today. Public education no longer teaches the responsibility that is necessary to articulate and defend fundamental rights, which includes owning property. Instead of owning property to secure one against poverty and government intrusion, now one must surrender principal ownership and pay rent to the government to *legally possess* property, all by force, for the sake of a collectivist philosophy. This is not to say that sound policy should not be established to regulate commercial property, and some personal property, for example, for public safety, against thieves, and corrupt people in business. I am strictly referring to privately owned, and necessarily basic property, which was designed by the Framers too not only keep government at bay, but to secure people within the basic necessities of their existence. Commercial property is something entirely different.

The founders understood quite clearly that if private property were subject to government oversight or regulations, then property value and its true ownership would decline into *serfdom.* Thus, the founders constructed the Constitution and its Rule of Law accordingly, which established an array of property rights provisions that are permanent and fixed. James Madison specifically makes this point, which is why education of one's rights is so important to property ownership, and why the fundamental right of property ownership is specifically secured as a way to keep government out of the individual's private life. Madison refers to this government oversight, or secondary laws designed to regulate private property ownership, as *mutable policy.*

> "The internal effects of a mutable policy are still more calamitous. It poisons the blessings of liberty itself. It will be of little avail to the people that the laws are made by men of their choice if the laws be so voluminous that they cannot be read, or so incoherent that they cannot be understood; if they be repealed or revised before they are promulgated, or undergo such incessant changes that no man, who knows what the law is today, can guess what it will be tomorrow. Law is defined to be a rule of action; but how can that be a rule, which is little known, and less fixed?"[3]

Mutable policies are secondary laws, also called *statutes*, which change over time and are a lawful means to regulate legal privileges. Primary Law is the Constitution, also called the Rule of Law. Statutes, however, are not a *lawful* means to regulate the free exercise of fundamental rights arbitrarily, like basic private property ownership, or the property itself, unless the right is no longer a fundamental right. This is exactly what property law does today, makes regulations on private property ownership "calamitous," whereby such laws "poison liberty," and these laws today are "so voluminous that they cannot be read, or so incoherent that they cannot be understood." This is, in part, and again, why education was so important to the founders. As Jefferson said,

> "I know no safe depository of the ultimate powers of the society but the people themselves, and if we think them not enlightened enough to exercise their control with a wholesome discretion, **the remedy is not to take it from them, but to inform their discretion by education. This is the true corrective of abuses of constitutional power."**[4] (bold added)

This is not to say, however, that such permanent provisions in the Law do not allow reflection upon changes over time, like within the increase of technology and social customs. These changes happen through juries and sound precedent, in part, and not directly by centralized power or by unelected bureaucrats. Most importantly however, juries, for example, are restricted also to specificity, as are judges, and are likewise limited by these permanent and fixed provisions within the actual Law. A jury, for instance, cannot convict an individual of a crime where there is a reasonable doubt.

Throughout most of the history of the world, a king or a dictator had always owned all property, in absolute. The people only had *legal possession* of property, and in England, for example, people had to pay rent to the King to simply live on the land and to live in their homes. If the legal possessors did not pay the King his rent, he took their property by force and either jailed or executed them, using his armed minions. This forced monopoly on absolute property ownership by a central power in English history derives from *William the Conqueror* in the 11th Century, who created an excessive *property tax* as a means to increase the power and wealth of the Monarchy. Later on, once the *divine rights of kings* was overruled by an English civil war between the Monarchy and Parliament, the Whig intellectuals, like Locke, expounded upon property rights, which greatly influenced the founders. Thus, America was to be very different, as it related to property ownership. In America, the individual could now truly own property, like a King, absent the consent or forced supervision of an overlord or by *mutable policy*. In addition, *absolute* ownership of private property, like a house or land, was something the founders established in America that has been circumvented by neo-progressive policy over time, for the sake of a collectivist philosophy. Absolute ownership means absolute control, and that the owner does not pay a king to keep living on their land or in their home through a property tax, or *quit-rent*. Quit-rent is something that Kings created and demanded from people who are *subjects* and not free. Non-free people cannot own property in absolute. Jefferson argued that the United States government would not participate in the traditional *rights of kings* over private land and property ownership,

"That we shall at this time also take notice of an error in the nature of our landholdings, which crept in at a very early period of our settlement. The introduction of the feudal tenures into the kingdom of England, though ancient, is well enough understood to set this matter in its proper light. In the earlier ages of the Saxon settlement feudal holdings were certainly altogether unknown, and very few, if any, had been introduced at the time of the Norman conquest. **Our Saxon ancestors held their lands, as they did their personal property, in absolute dominion, disencumbered with any superior. . . . William the Conqueror first introduced that system [feudalism] generally.** The lands which had belonged to those who fell at the battle of Hastings, and in the subsequent insurrections of his reign, formed a considerable proportion of the lands of the whole kingdom. These he granted out, subject to feudal duties, as did he also those of a great number of his new subjects, who by persuasions or threats were induced to surrender then for that purpose. But still much of the land was left in the hands of his Saxon subjects, held of no superior, and not subject to feudal conditions. . . . A general principle indeed was introduced that "all lands in England were held either mediately or immediately of the crown": but thus was borrowed from those holdings which were truly feudal, and applied to others for the purposes of illustration. Feudal holdings were therefore but exceptions out of the Saxon laws of possession, under which all lands were held in absolute right. These

therefore still form the basis of the common law, to prevail whenever the exceptions have not taken place. **America was not conquered by William the Norman, nor its lands surrendered to him or any of his successors. Possessions are undoubtedly of the [absolute disencumbered] nature. Our ancestors however, were laborers, not lawyers. The fictitious principle that all lands belong originally to the king, that they were early persuaded to believe real, and accordingly took grants of their own lands from the crown. And while the crown continued to grant for small sums and on reasonable rents, there was no inducement to arrest the error."**[5] (bold added)

Jefferson here is referring to the King no longer holding such absolute power or ownership over the lands in the Colonies, whereby the colonies had to pay property taxes or *quit- rent* to the King to legally possess and live on the land, or in their homes. Jefferson said that such a government financial scheme, as "feudal duties," would not take place in America. Why do we still hold to this convention of quit-rent at the local level?

Under the *Treaty of Paris,* American lands were given over to the Colonies in *Allodium.* Allodium means absolute ownership, absent and free of any obligations to a higher authority. Black's Law Dictionary 2nd Edition, defines allodium as, "Land held absolutely in one's own right, and not of any lord or superior; land not subject to feudal duties or burdens. An estate held by absolute ownership, without recognizing any superior to whom any duty is due on account thereof." But here is where the government silently encroaches upon *period terms* to socially engineer the people away from such rights and knowledge of absolute property ownership, as is complimented by such terms. The 2nd Edition of Black's Law Dictionary was written during the 18th Century and reflects the most competent understanding of the legal language at that time. However, when one looks at the more modern legal jargon, as with the newer 8th Edition of Black's Law Dictionary, the term allodium changes very subtly to transition absolute ownership into the limits of *fee simple* title. The 8th addition reads that allodium is, "An estate held in fee simple absolute." Then look up *Fee Simple* in the same 8th Edition, it reads that Fee Simple is, "An interest in land that, being the broadest property interest allowed by law." Isn't "allowed by law" a superior? What does the definition mean by "interest?" What happened to the words, *right* or *feudal duties or burdens* from the earlier definition? *Allodium* doesn't really exist anymore. That is what happened. When a government or entity owns all land and property in absolute and rents that land or property to people for a fee or a tax, these obligatory payments are called *feudal duties,* said Jefferson. Paying such fees on property you "own" is also a type of soft *Feudalism,* absent the middlemen originally called *noblemen.* America was not to be Feudal, at all, again, as Jefferson asserted above. Well what does *feudal duties* mean today? Feudal duties simply means a fee paid on property under obligation to a higher authority, or as it was called under a King, *quit-rent.* Do you pay your local government annual feudal duties to live on land you "own"? Do you pay your local government annual quit-rent to live in a house you "own?" Do you pay the government an annual property tax to drive in a car you "own?" "Oh," the neo-progressives cry out, "The times have changed. How do we pay to keep you safe and secure? How do we pay to educate our youth?" Just because the government cuts out the *noble classes* today as the *middle-man,* in acquiring property tax revenue as feudal duties, does not change the fact that the government still collects feudal duties, or quit-rent, by force, on property you think you own. The nobles themselves, at the time, and as much as today, paid feudal duties by force to a *superior* also. They simply turned around and took it by force from the peasants (poor people). So what has changed really? Thus, enforcement worked the same then as it does today. On a side note, I recall when closing on my own house, I asked the lawyer what he thought of Allodial title, in comparison to Fee Simple title. He looked at me lost for a sec, and said he didn't know what I was talking about, and that he had never heard of Allodial title. He went back to pointing to where my signatures were needed on the three party contracts.

I want to emphasize here that this absolute, or allodial ownership of property by an individual is soundly temporary, "A power to dispose of estates for ever is manifestly absurd. The earth and the fullness of it belongs to every generation, and the preceding one can have no right to bind it up from posterity. Such extension of property is quite unnatural." Here Thomas Jefferson is echoing the mind of Adam Smith, as it relates to sound capitalism and property ownership.[6] Allodium is only *reasonable* during one's own lifetime. Likewise, I am neither advocating an abolishment of property tax. The founders did agree that it was a necessary and a collective, public effort to fund government, in part, and public education through a *limited* property tax. Jefferson made the remark to Madison, for example, that those, "who can find uncultivated land, shall be at liberty to cultivate it, paying a moderate rent."[6.5] Cultivating lands were also generally of a commercial enterprise. Property tax is very necessary for certain areas of government to function. However, there needs to be limits, and the founders did set limits. Limits then are not within the same context of what government redefines limits as today, however.

As it relates to funding education, for example, from property taxes, John Adams said, "The whole people must take upon themselves the education of the whole people and be willing to bear the expenses of it...there should not be a district of one mile square, without a school in it, not founded by a charitable individual, but maintained at the public expense of the people themselves."[7] Thomas Jefferson also emphasized that public tax revenue shall be the funding source for public education,

> "I think by far the most important bill in our whole code is that for the diffusion of knowledge among the people. No other sure foundation can be devised, for the preservation of freedom and happiness...my dear Sir, a crusade against ignorance; establish & improve the law for educating the common people. Let our countrymen know that the people alone can protect us against these evils [tyranny, oppression, etc.] and **that the tax which will be paid for this purpose is not more than the thousandth part of what will be paid to kings, priests and nobles who will rise up among us if we leave the people in ignorance."[8]**

How do we as Americans from the future reconcile this charge of the founders to publicly fund education and other necessary government functions, through property tax revenue, with the equal and sound charge that, "No power on earth has a right to take our property from us without our consent." said John Jay, the first Chief Justice of the United States, who was quoting Locke. Today, neo-progressives will argue the ideology of *implied consent* in the legislatures. This has only undermined protections like *allodium,* however. What do Benjamin Franklin and Thomas Jefferson both say about a real and private property tax? The framers put a sound and lawful solution into place, to remedy this very squabble, as a way to secure people not only from government intrusion, but to also secure people from extreme poverty and homelessness.

But first, and most importantly, property ownership meant personal liberty. Property ownership meant independence and property ownership meant limited government, which secured personal privacy. Property ownership also meant security from extreme poverty. Today, when an individual wants to purchase real property, for example, somehow, someway, government bureaucracy gets involved in the process, thus nullifying from the start, ownership as a way to limit government from being intimately involved in one's personal life. In addition, and sadly so, the individual is actually freer today by not "owning" property, because not owning property keeps government at bay. So what happened to American republicanism? Well, very basically, American Government became a big business, a *corporation,*[9] run by banks, CEOs and big business minded politicians who wanted to capitalize on private property and increase government revenue by controlling and attaching monetary value to any and everything under the sun, which in turn increased government power over any and everything associated with an individual's life. Have you ever met your *strawman?* In 1816, Thomas Jefferson warned his friend George Logan in a letter, that what destroys a country morally is when big business becomes a source to create law. From this, government creates and secures aristocracy, that such corporations must be "crushed" before they become powerful enough to determine the workings of government. Today, big American business makes law, contrary to the founders' intent. Making reference to England as the example of this, Jefferson wrote,

> "The man who is dishonest as a statesman would be a dishonest man in any station....In this respect England exhibits the most remarkable phaenomenon in the universe in the contrast between the profligacy of its government and the probity of its citizens. And accordingly it is now exhibiting an example of the truth of the maxim that virtue & interest are inseparable. It ends, as might have been expected, in the ruin of it's people, but this ruin will fall heaviest, as it ought to fall on that hereditary aristocracy which has for generations been preparing the catastrophe. I hope we shall take warning from the example and crush in it's birth the aristocracy of our monied corporations which dare already to challenge our government to a trial of strength and bid defiance to the laws of our country."[10]

Corporations here are a bit different than corporations today, but are essentially the same. Corporation in Jefferson's time meant *commercial enterprise*. Combine this business mindedness in government with a collectivist philosophy and corporatism is born. Corporatism is when everything has a price, is regulated by statutes and all property belongs to the government, to everybody else in legal possession only, by force, with the dollar at the center. In a recent, well-written article by Jim Sleeper at Salon, he noted that *We the People* in mass are to blame for allowing this, "A liberal capitalist republic has to rely on its citizens to uphold voluntarily certain public virtues and beliefs that neither the liberal state nor markets can nourish or defend." The term "liberal" is not necessarily referring to liberal in the contemporary, political sense, but of the classical "freedom" sense, also called *Classical Liberalism*, of which I favor. What we are experiencing now as the failings of our principled republic, are actually symptoms of the laziness and ignorance of the people in general,

> "Having miscarried republican self-discipline and conviction so badly, we find ourselves scrambling to monitor, measure and control the consequences, such as the proliferation of mental illness and the glorification and marketing of guns, as if these were causing our implosion. They aren't. They're symptoms, not causes — reactions to widespread heartbreak at the breakdown of what Tocqueville called republican habits of the heart that we used to cultivate. Equally symptomatic, not causal, are self-avowedly "deviant" and "transgressive" gyrations by people who

imagine that the sunset of civic-republican order heralds a liberating, Dionysian dawn. Sloughing off our bad old repressions, we've been swept up by the swift market currents that turn countercultures into over-the-counter cultures and promote a free-for-all that's a free-for-none as citizens become customers chasing "freedoms" for sale. Even our war-makers' and -mongers' grand strategies and the growing militarization of our domestic police forces are more symptomatic than causal of the public derangement that's rising all around us."[11]

In the end, the fundamental rights of individual liberty and absolute ownership of basic and necessary property, as established at the founding, and which is still the *Law of the Land,* ironically, proved not to be good for big government business, unless government has absolute control. Moreover, this *new style* of economic progress, secured in statutes, has digressed society away from the property protections secured in the Law of the Land, back into a type of aristocracy and soft feudalism, as was in England prior to American Independence. These statutes that secure this new style of economic progress have now become the law in law enforcement.

What is Property?

It is important to define property and to define ownership. Unfortunately today, government redefines what property is and redefines what ownership is through property law, or secondary laws, and based upon the property's value and/or the property's purpose. This continually evolves, like with Black's Law Dictionary redefining the term *Allodium*. Similarly, the terms *property* and *ownership* have undergone many "legal" revisions, thus changing the definition of what ownership is for its "reasonable" control and valuation. Recall that property ownership was to be radically different then in past governments, especially and specifically from the English Monarchy. In establishing property rights in America, the founders understood how connected such a right is to individual liberty and autonomy, compared to historical views of what property ownership meant and actually was. How can a king, or despot own property absolutely and not a common person? Because, the king had an army that could legally commit acts of violence, at the King's will, and simply by the King decreeing that any such violence executed in his name was law. Moreover, common people, all people as a matter of fact, were unequal to the King.

As aforementioned, Jefferson emphasized, by nature, land is not actually attached to an individual beyond that individual's lifetime, therefore absolute ownership is *reasonable*. Furthermore, part of progressing out of a monarchy, where people had to pay a tax to the king, law should secure the individual on their land for that *moment* of their existence, as *stable* ownership. Jefferson reiterates,

"It is a moot question whether the origin of any kind of property is derived from nature at all... It is agreed by those who have seriously considered the subject that no individual has, of natural right, a separate property in an acre of land, for instance. By an universal law, indeed, whatever, whether fixed or movable, belongs to all men equally and in common is the property for the moment of him who occupies it; but when he relinquishes the occupation, the property goes with it. Stable ownership is the gift of social law, and is given late in the progress of society."[12]

All land, in its natural origin, and until owned by an individual, is owned by humanity as a whole. And, as it relates to *public property,* for example, parks, schools, religious sites, and the like, are always owned in common, or collectively, by the citizens within a specific jurisdiction. *Private property,* however, is not. This is the difference in universal and social law. The new American government is lawfully charged to secure the *real* and private property ownership of individuals, again, as the sign of sound progression out of European aristocracy. Prior to the establishment of the United States, Jefferson makes reference to this by citing the Native Americans owning land in common prior to American progress within society as a whole, whereby individual land ownership is protected by law,

"A right of property in moveable things is admitted before the establishment of government. A separate property in lands, not till after that establishment. The right to moveables is acknowledged by all the hordes of Indians surrounding us. Yet by no one of them has a separate property in lands been yielded to individuals. He who plants a field keeps possession till he has gathered the produce, after which one has as good a right as another to occupy it. Government must be established and laws provided, before lands can be separately appropriated, and their owner protected in his possession. Till then, the property is in the body of the nation, and they, or their chief as trustee, must grant them to individuals, and determine the conditions of the grant."[13]

Today, property law has become unbelievably complicated in an effort for government to redefine *property, ownership,* and *legal possession.* Also, this has slippery sloped into the creation of new terms, all designed to legally connect government intimately to private property, economically and socially, above and beyond the individual. *Blight* and *zoning* are a few terms that come to mind that are heavily abused, but can be reasonably necessary. The argument against an individual today truly owning property is a collectivist argument, which principally reasons that governments must use quit-rent from any and all real and private property as a way to fund public services. Such intended complications within property law are not only necessary to secure such a system, but have, over time, transformed the founders' view of property ownership back into the pre-American philosophy of Hobbes', that all property shall be owned in common, whereby the people in government hold absolute ownership, just as the King did before we declared Independence. Try to purchase some land directly from another individual absent a lawyer and absent government bureaucracy. It won't happen because the government today owns all the land. Oh they argue that such bureaucracy is for your protection one way or another, but is it really? The lawyer is there because the laws are overly complicated and need to be interpreted and explained. Bureaucracy is there to make sure that true ownership is secured for the government and that the individuals are limited to *legal possession* of the property. I'm pretty sure property laws today are not what Jefferson had in mind when he talked about laws protecting property rights. If Americans still truly owned property in principal, there would be far less need for lawyers and surely less need for bureaucracy, leading to less government, which in turn would cause great inconveniences for government. And there in lies part of the problem. The irony is, this very thinking sounds ludicrous today to most people because most people have been slowly, over time, conditioned away from absolute property ownership. Thus the term, "wards of the court."

Neo-progressives argue the need for property co-ownership between government and individuals because most people are incapable of exercising the responsibility associated with principal property ownership. This may be somewhat reasonable, but only because people have not been educated and cultivated into such responsibility. Big government ideas need big funding, which could not happen if people really owned their property. Property ownership is a fundamental, natural right, and it is because of unsound, secondary laws, derivative of unsound precedent, that such a right is thwarted for the purpose of securing principal ownership for only the government. Government is just an entity, made up of other humans.

Government cannot actually own anything, but a human can, within their lifetime. In addition, Jefferson declared it immoral and unjust that government takes property by force for the purpose of *redistribution,* that only true owners may use force to take property stolen by thieves, for example, and not government for its own purposes, "By nature's law, every man has a right to seize and retake by force his own property taken from him by another by force or fraud. Nor is this natural right among the first which is taken into the hands of regular government after it is instituted."[14] So when government is the principal owner of property, it becomes the principal executioner of force in securing that ownership. You are the co-owner.

On that note, the Courts have made it clear that income is property, *James vs. The United States,* 970 F.2d 750 (10th Cir. 1992). Thus, the *income tax* can actually be viewed as a property tax on one's labor and income, absent due process, but by way of the contract. Some argue that the income tax is an excise tax, or duty, since the Federal Reserve owns the currency, and whereby the *Apportionment Clause* in the Constitution must apply. Either way, and in the end, redefining money and not defining *income*, is why the government had to amend the Constitution, for its own sake, to *get around* the Due Process of Law requirement in the 5th and 14th Amendments, and to *get around* or circumvent the permanent and fixed provisions designed originally to secure property rights in absolute, like the right to earn a living.

Are owning socks the same thing as owning a tractor? No. Why not? Because, the people in government can tax the tractor's value, not socks. Plus socks are inside the home, which is still protected by the 4th Amendment, for now. One loophole governments have created to get around the 4th Amendment is to associate property inside the home with economic activity. So if you earn income from within your home, depending on the jurisdiction, the government can tax the property you use to earn that income. As it relates to the outside of the home, you don't truly own the tractor because if you don't pay the tax, the people in government can use their monopoly on violence, law enforcement, to come take it, and resell it for currency, to make up for the tax. They can't do that with socks, because socks hold no value. Frederick Bastiat, in his most famous book simply called *The Law,* where he specifically and intentionally argued against Marxism and the redistribution of wealth by force, calls this act of taxation *legal plundering:*

> "Now, legal plunder can be committed in an infinite number of ways. Thus we have an infinite number of plans for organizing it: tariffs, protection, benefits, subsidies, encouragements, progressive taxation, public schools, guaranteed jobs, guaranteed profits, minimum wages, a right to relief, a right to the tools of labor, free credit, and so on, and so on."

Again, what does it mean today to own something? Is owning your car the same thing as owning your shovel? How about land? Is owning land today the same thing as owning your house? Or better yet, is owning land today the same as owning land two hundred years ago? As society advances and populations increase, many people in government argue the need for more revenue by forcefully taxing and redistributing people's property and wealth to fund more social controls and more social programs, and to fund more bureaucracy and enforcement to implement those programs and controls. Such controls are designed not only to control behavior, but also to control the use of property, which is why the government makes itself the principal owner, to make controlling your property "legal." Today, secondary laws that are designed to control the use of property are written in such a complicated way as to secure the government's maximum authority. What about maximum liberty for the individual? In *Pennell vs. City of San Jose,* the US Supreme Court explained, as it relates to the city's control of rent, that such controls attract politicians because it imposes costs onto the property owners, which, "permit wealth transfers...to be achieved 'off budget,' with relative invisibility and thus relative immunity from normal democratic processes." In short, this scheme is far easier than asking the people to vote on whether or not the city should use taxpayer money to help pay people's rent.

The whole purpose of property rights, which secures true property ownership, is to also protect the minority from the will of the majority. This was one of the greatest challenges, or prerogatives, of the new American government. This is one reason, in part, why Madison argues for a Bill of Rights, "Another happy effect of this prerogative would be its control on the internal vicissitudes of State policy; and the aggressions of interested majorities on the rights of minorities and of individuals."[15] The will of the majority cannot overrule the property rights of the minority, thus the Bill of Rights protects the minority against what most people want. Our foremost foundational principles, as it relates to property, derive from the philosophy of John Locke. It was Locke who paved the way and advanced the building blocks for American property ownership. Not only philosophically, but socially and economically. Locke emphasized three aspects of human freedom that are separate from law, separate from government and separate from other people: "life, liberty and property." Locke also argued that, "the individual ownership of goods and property is justified by the labor exerted to produce those goods or utilize property to produce goods beneficial to human society,"[16] that property precedes government and government cannot "dispose of the estates of the subjects arbitrarily."[17] Yet politicians today think that their primary job is to create and sustain government revenue at the expense of property rights.

The later political philosophy of Karl Marx heavily criticized Locke's view of property and plays a profound role in the neo-progressive view of property today. One thing is for sure, it was Locke's view of property that inspired our founding fathers to make property ownership central to liberty in America. It was Thomas Jefferson who took Locke's view of property and absorbed it into what it means to *pursue happiness,* thus changing the foundational liberty premise of Locke in the Declaration of Independence to, "life, liberty and the pursuit of happiness." Private property ownership, according to the founders, was not necessarily about the possessions or the goods themselves, but that those possessions are the result of a manifestation of the fundamental right to pursue happiness.[18] "The first principles of association" says Jefferson, is "the guarantee to everyone of a free exercise of his industry, and the fruits acquired by it."[19] Yet this fundamental right to own property, which includes income, as a primary aspect of the pursuit of happiness, has been slowly eroded by *legal plundering*. Without private property ownership, wrote James Wilson, one of the authors of the US Constitution, "the tranquility of society would be perpetually disturbed by fierce and ungovernable competitions for the possession and enjoyment of things, insufficient to satisfy all, and by no rule of adjustment distributed by each."[20] This is what is happening today through *forced fairness* and the *redistribution of wealth*. The government creates big problems by trying to fix small ones. Property rights are essential to preserving the individual right to pursue happiness as well as the collective right to preserve peace and happiness within society as a whole, thus Madison said, "The personal right to acquire property, which is a natural right, gives to property, when acquired, a right to protection, as a social right."[21]

Over the past century or so, the courts, and law enforcement as well, have continually deviated from their original purpose, which is, in part, to protect individuals from arbitrary legislation. Or, to put it another way, the Judicial Branch should protect people from the Executive and Legislative Branches, or the Executive Branch should protect people from the Legislative and Judicial Branches. Nonetheless, the collectivist effort has undermined individual property rights and has set false precedent in the courts by actually, again, redefining terms. Precedent, for example, has redefined the 5th Amendment's *public use* in the *Kelo vs. New London* case, where the Supreme Court ruled that local governments could take private property and give it to private developers. Again, this comes down to philosophy, an ideology adopted by individuals in government who then consciously work against the vivacity of their Oath, for the sake of America as a corporation, a big business. Dissenting in the *Kelo* case, Justice Sandra Day O'Connor wrote, "Under the banner of economic development, all private property is now vulnerable to being taken and transferred to another private owner.... The founders cannot have intended this perverse result." Again, our founders, based upon Locke's philosophy of liberty, designed the American Rule of Law to protect and secure individual property rights from the will of the majority, and especially from the arbitrary will of those in government. The majority throughout history has had some say in public policy, and it still should, to some degree. Yet, not as it relates to undermining fundamental rights like owning property. So if eighty one percent of the population wants to take an individual's land so that a Wal-Mart can be built to create jobs, the majority cannot lawfully do it. Why not? Because, in America, property rights are fundamental to personal liberty, which was the whole intention of gaining Independence from an English Monarchy, where all property is feudalistic and owned by the King. Property is the extension of an individual's labor. Labor itself is one's own property. The self is property and what labor creates is property, which is actualizing the "pursuit of happiness" that Jefferson talks about. People today are being conditioned that secondary laws regulate legal possession of property by force, or, even whether or not the individual can own or be in legal possession of property, like a plant. Jefferson makes the point, "He who is permitted by law to have no property of his own can with difficulty conceive that property is founded in anything but force."[22]

The Rule of Law is designed to prevent the people in government and people within a majority of the population from violating the rights of other people. The

Constitution only works correctly, as a single power, when the letter and the spirit of the Law are adhered to and enforced. The very idea of the majority agreeing to take one individual's land for the benefit of a private company, to create jobs, is a violation of the landowner's property rights, plain and simple. The *Public Use* clause in the 5th Amendment to the US Constitution is not a means to manipulate an argument to sidestep this protection legally. Public use is *public use,* not *private use* for public use. Locke emphasized that freedom is not the absence of law, but rather freedom is to be preserved through law,

> "The end of law is not to abolish or restrain, but to preserve and enlarge freedom.... For liberty means, to be free from restraint and violence from others; which cannot be, where there is no law: (for who could be free, when every other man's humour might domineer over him?) but a liberty to dispose, and order as he lists, his person, actions, possessions, and his whole property, within the allowance of those laws under which he is, and there in not to be subject to the arbitrary will of another, but freely follow his own."[23]

Well then how is taking an individual's land for the sake of creating jobs in the community arbitrary, and not for public use? Because public use is predicated upon government sustainability, and, whereby tax revenue is the financial source for such sustainability. A Wal- Mart is privately owned for private profit. Public use property is collectively owned, like a park or a library, which are sustained by tax revenue. In reality, the ulterior motive for such a scheme like *Kelo,* is that the more jobs that are created equals more income tax revenue for the state and the federal government, and an increase in sales tax revenue at the state and local levels. There is always an ulterior motive and it is usually money and power, also known as *greed in action.* Attached to this greed is a nice benevolent argument. The government didn't support women in the work force, for example, because of *equality,* no. The government encouraged women into the workforce because it literally doubled income tax revenue. That is a fact. Prior to this, women raised children at home and instilled in them life's fundamentals. Now the government gets in there at an early age and instills "fundamentals" like being a good worker and obeying authority, and they do it because women are at work now. This is not a critique of working women at all, but a statement of *a posteriori* fact.[23.5]

James Madison wrote in his essay called *Property,* which sums up Locke's view, "Government is instituted to protect property of every sort; as well that which lies in the various rights of individuals, as that which the term particularly expresses. This being the end of government, that alone is a just government, which *impartially* secures to every man, whatever is his *own.*" Where does this transfer of private property to private ownership by force, which benefits public use, and by the courts, come from? *Wickard vs. Filburn.* This case is a prime example of not only how the government transfers private property to private property for public use by force, but this case is a primary example of the manipulation of the language of the *Commerce Clause,* which justified the taking of a man's wheat from his farm, thus creating very bad "legal" precedent and nullifying the farmer's property rights. Moreover, this case has slippery sloped into a war on raw foods and dairy, as a means to disseminate the corporate food system, which of course generates tax revenue. The icing on the cake is the good ol' trusty "public safety" arguments combined with the sweet justification of citing secondary legislation.

Hobbes, contrary to Locke, argued against the idea of individual property rights. Hobbes was arguing for the *divine right of kings,* specifically rationalizing the rule of King Charles II. Hobbes said that if people owned private property, it would lead to the devastation of civilized society and return the people to a *State of Nature*, a nature of warfare,

> "A fifth doctrine that tendeth to the dissolution of a Commonwealth is that every private man has an absolute propriety in his goods, such as excludeth the right of the sovereign. Every man has indeed a propriety that excludes the right of every other subject: and he has it only from the sovereign power, without the protection whereof every other man should have right to the same. But the right of the sovereign also be excluded, he cannot perform the office they have put him into, which is to defend them both from foreign enemies and from the injuries of one another; and consequently there is no longer a Commonwealth."[24]

In the end, Hobbes said that if people truly owned private property, it would limit government's ability to protect people from themselves and from foreign invasion. Therefore, Hobbes said, in short, that government should hold absolute, central power over the masses, who are easily manipulated, and who are generally dim-witted and easily subject to violence. Sound familiar? Isn't this America today? Yet historically, governments respond to violence with violence, so what has changed? Like I said before, it comes down to the philosophical views of individuals who either believe or who do not believe in property rights and personal liberty. Sadly, there are many who are employed in American government today who simply do not like what the founders stood for. But it is not up to those who do not believe in property rights and personal liberty. The American Rule of Law that secures these fundamentals has already been established. And, those who seek to change it stomp on and spit in the face of those who have died for such principles. These people who seek to undermine our Rule of Law from within are *neo-progressives.* When these types of government officials undermine property rights through the legal system, they do so because the people not in government let them.

The Law

The US Constitution secures and protects the free individual's property ownership from the will of the majority and from the arbitrary will of the people in government within three of first ten Amendments called the Bill of Rights, as a matter of Law and not as a matter of policy. The Third and Fourth Amendments were designed to protect people's homes from forceful entry and the stationing of military personnel, which was heavily abused in the Colonies by King George the III. The Fourth Amendment reads,

> "The right of the people **to be secure in their persons, houses, papers, and effects, against unreasonable searches and seizures, shall not be violated,** and no Warrants shall issue, but upon probable cause, supported by Oath or affirmation, and particularly describing the place to be searched, and the persons or things to be seized." (bold added)

Notice how strong the 4th Amendment language is, "...shall not be violated?" When law enforcement reasonably suspects a person of having committed a crime, they must find *probable cause* and submit the evidence for review to a judicial official, followed by that judge's/magistrate's approval and signature, in order to secure a warrant. This must be done before a cop can arrest and/or use *force* against the suspect and their property, unless the crime is actually witnessed by the officer. In addition, the warrant must be specific as to the area to be searched and the property to be seized. How certain are we, however, that the magistrate is not being complicit with law enforcement, as to what the lack of probable cause may be within any specific request for a warrant? A magistrate may very well be easily persuaded into issuing a warrant simply by rhetoric within the context of the officer's articulation of what counts as probable cause, for them, or by way of a statute's dictatorial command to issue a warrant in specific circumstances. *Officer articulation* is extremely important and can be a double-edged sword, depending upon the individual officer's moral compass and constitutional comprehension. Is the judicial official unbiased? Is the cop unbiased? Are the judicial official and the cop's understanding of probable cause founded upon their understanding of the Constitution itself, or is their understanding of what probable cause is based upon their *training*? Or, is their understanding founded upon a combination of both? The latter is more reasonable. Still, one must surrender to one or the other, ultimately. Therefore, conviction of one over the other must derive from knowledge, not necessarily by training. Training and education are not equal. Many times law enforcement officials do not request a search warrant when certain magistrates are on duty. They wait for the one that may easily issue the warrant. This is called *magistrate shopping.*

The 4th Amendment has its origin in the fact that King George III would allow individuals within his enforcement ranks to write their own search and seizure warrants, and then just go into people's homes and take their stuff at will, and on mere suspicion of criminal activity. Moreover, the King would create crime as a means to justify getting into people's homes and to take their stuff. For example, the Stamp Act. How do we, then, define what the term *unreasonable* means in the 4th Amendment? *Unreasonable* is defined within the

Amendment itself, which overall, is a search or seizure of an individual, their home or personal property absent a warrant founded upon probable cause. Well what is probable cause? Probable cause, according to Cornell Law School, is when there is a reasonable basis that a crime may have been committed and that specific evidence of the crime is present in the place to be searched. If evidence can be secured by way of *plain view,* absent a search or a seizure, then generally a warrant is not necessary. In spite of the Law, however, neo-progressive thinking, and even many law enforcement officials, in general, seek to manipulate this lawful process by articulating a mandate to search or seize property as a matter of policy instead of a matter of Law, because the Law itself is too restrictive upon the government's effort in catching the "bad guy." To illustrate, recently Robert S. Litt, general counsel for the Office of the Director of National Intelligence, which runs the NSA, corroborated this fact in counsel with the *Privacy and Civil Liberties Oversight Board,* by actually saying that finding probable cause on individuals to secure search warrants which would allow lawful surveillance of certain individuals is just "too difficult."[25] This "difficulty" then leads to *matters of policy* designed to circumvent the Amendment's provision by articulating, usually through thousands of pages of "legal" and pseudo-rational jargon, ways around the probable cause requirement and thus expanding such enforcement in general. The *Patriot Act,* or *Civil Asset Forfeiture* comes to mind. Secondary laws, in this regard, then, are created out of a *matter of policy* consensus, which are also ultimately *withstanding* to the Constitution. In the *rationale* of *Civil Asset Forfeiture,* for example, policy redefines and labels such enforcement as *civil,* and the property itself as the *defendant,* thus targeting the actual property as the criminal. Labeling the taking of personal property as *civil* allows cops to "legally" violate or circumvent the Law of the 4th Amendment. Or, as Bastiat called it, *legal plundering.* What about when the Legislative Branch criminalizes the possession of property for the purpose of adhering to specific interest groups? For example, the Brady Campaign's fight against the cosmetic appearance of certain types of guns. Is not a gun property first if not used as a weapon? Is not the Brady Campaign a special interest group? The NRA is not an interest group in my mind because it advocates the free exercise of a fundamental right. Rights are not special interests. The Brady Campaign seeks to work against such a right.

To be secure in one's *person* simply means that the cops cannot search or seize an individual without a warrant. A pat down, however, to search for weapons in the midst of *reasonable suspicion* of a possible crime is not a search.[26] Nor can the cops search a person's residence without a warrant. An individual's "papers and effects" can neither be searched nor seized without a warrant. "Effects" in the 4th Amendment means personal property, such as cell phones, computers, a toolbox, a vehicle, luggage, a purse and the like, unless quantified as a "pat down," which is not a search. None of which can be seized or searched without a warrant. That is the Law. A law enforcement officer generally must ask for permission, or consent, to search any personal property because if they get consent to search, the Constitution becomes null and void, for that moment, unless the individual retracts their consent. Yet, *public policy* can deem otherwise, and especially in the name of *terrorism, a state of emergency* or *exigent circumstances,* which are all later progressive manipulations of the case law, created as a means to avoid the restrictions of the Law on the people in government, for "public safety," purposes. These exceptions are commonly recognized by precedent, or case law (Katz v. U.S.). Public policy also incites and socially engineers officers to make reference to the judicial branch as the legal justification for their actions, when questioned by an individual about a search, as opposed to their own right of conscience and by the officer adhering to the simple language of the Constitution itself. A good example of this is the recent case of *Commonwealth of Pennsylvania vs. Shiem* (2014), in which the Pennsylvanian Supreme Court ruled that law enforcement no longer needs a warrant to search vehicles. A competent officer would still seek a warrant when the need to search a vehicle arises. An incompetent officer would readily search a car simply because the court said it was ok, thus withstanding to what the 4th Amendment actually reads. These are essentially ignorance and character issues in the incompetent officer. A police state can only come about when all three branches of government are complicit to one another. A police state is grossly unlawful and extremely un-American. These legal efforts to control property count as what Madison called, *silent encroachments.* These are small changes, as a matter of policy (mutable policy), over time, that in the end usurp the Law. The Constitution only allows *Treason,* for example, to be the only crime not completely subject to 4th Amendment protection, adding that testimony itself from two witnesses, or by confession, must be in addition to whatever evidence is secured against the defendant. In short, absent two witnesses or confession, a person cannot be convicted of treason, even though the evidence to the contrary may be overwhelming. However, in the spirit of past despots, to get around this, the definition of Treason merely needs to be expanded on to encompass the controls the government wants. Fortunately, the founders foresaw such a likely abuse and specifically defined Treason and how it shall commence further. In the Constitution itself, Article 3, Section 3, reads,

> Treason against the United States, shall consist only in levying War against them, or in adhering to their Enemies, giving them Aid and Comfort. **No Person shall be convicted of Treason unless on the Testimony of two Witnesses to the same overt Act, or on Confession in open Court.** The Congress shall have Power to declare the Punishment of Treason, but no Attainder of Treason shall work Corruption of Blood, or Forfeiture except during the Life of the Person attainted. (bold added)

This is very important because such a specific definition prevents government officials from adhocing the term, or redefining the term *treason,* as a way to actualize an agenda, or to justify the actions against a specific target. The word "levying" may be another issue. As we have seen throughout American legal history, *adhocing* is a philosophical process where someone tries to prevent the falsification of an argument that has been created as an attempt to rationalize changes made to the original terms of the argument. For example, the term *ownership* has been adhoced into the term *legal possession* as a means for government to maximize and justify government authority over what it means to own something, while still utilizing the term "ownership."

The next Amendment within the Bill of Rights that protects property ownership is the 5th Amendment, which reads,

> "No person shall be held to answer for a capital, or otherwise infamous crime, unless on a presentment or indictment of a Grand Jury, except in cases arising in the land or naval forces, or in the Militia, when in actual service in time of War or public danger; nor shall any person be subject for the same offense to be twice put in jeopardy of life or limb; nor shall be compelled in any criminal case to be a witness against himself, **nor be deprived of life, liberty, or property, without due process of law; nor shall private property be taken for public use, without just compensation."** (bold added)

"No person shall be...deprived of life, liberty, or property, without due process..." These are the fundamental, *inalienable rights* that Locke, in his political dissertation, said are natural and are beyond the arbitrary rule of government. The founders agreed and made it the *Law of the Land,* whereby such infringement of these rights by government would be subject to very strict rules. *Due Process* of law comes out of the Magna Carta, which declares, "No freeman shall be taken, or imprisoned, or disseised, or outlawed, or exiled, or in any way harmed - nor will we go upon or send him - save by lawful judgment of his peers or by the Law of the Land." *Due Process* basically means that an individual can have their day in court, whereby as the defendant, they can cross-examine their accuser and the accuser's witnesses. As a defendant, they can also submit evidence on their own behalf. And, most importantly, as it relates to due process, the burden of proof falls upon the government, which must be beyond a reasonable doubt. It is here, in the 5th Amendment, that I believe the Supreme Court seriously flawed in its interpretation of *public use* in the *Kelo* case. *Public use* can, arbitrarily, just about substantiate any and all arguments for taking private property. This is another example of adhocing. Madison said, "In framing a government which is to be administered by men over men, the great difficulty lies in this: you must first enable the government to control the governed; and in the next place oblige it to control itself."[27] Thus, the Law, or Constitution was designed, for example, to determine the act of theft equally for the people in government as it is defined for the people not in government. To steal is to steal, period. Assault is assault, period. Policies like *Qualified Immunity* have then been created as a means to rationalize, or adhoc, the government's ability to commit crime in the midst of preventing, stopping or solving crime.

Blackstonian Theory

A great dichotomy has slowly arisen in the courts between the intended Constitutional protections of private property ownership and the neo-progressive legal precedent that slowly usurps these "difficult" protections. Similar to the original views that helped establish the principles in the Constitution, this dichotomy also has a history in political philosophy. Let's face it, there are people in and out of government who simply do not believe in private property ownership, or property rights in general. They believe that all property should be owned in common and that any and all property should be allocated and controlled by a centralized power, in such a way that benefits the *common good* as a whole. It sounds nice, but in practice, such a philosophical view would undermine the entire American Revolution, and the Declaration of Independence. Moreover, such a view in practice not only blends modern America into the likeness of other collectivist countries, it would also return the United States to the historical authoritarianism of 18th Century England, where the people in government were unequal to the people not in government, and all property was owned and controlled by one central power, the King.

Locke believed that government should be limited to the natural, moral law, as common individuals ought to be. This is, again, and in part, why the founders adopted Locke's political philosophy to create the American system of government, which is "centralized" in the US Constitution and the Declaration of Independence. If it is wrong for an individual to murder, steal or violate the fundamental rights of others, then it is also equally wrong for government to murder, steal and violate the rights of others. Government power is limited to a natural, moral law and to the people's fundamental rights. In addition, again, rights derive from property, first and foremost, and primarily from self-ownership. If natural, moral law is not the foundation of just government, then what is? If this is not the case, then people in government can legitimately rationalize any and all activity within government. In opposition to Locke, there are an array of philosophical views for thinking the contrary of what has become fundamentally the case in America. Hobbes's view was just one example. There is another such view, and many people in American government, in the past and today, consciously and subconsciously, hold to this view, and they hold to this view specifically for the reason of justifying any and all government activity, which has become secured in *precedent.*

Sir William Blackstone, an English jurist, judge and politician, who published the *Commentaries on the Laws of England* in the 1760s, had a profound effect on legal minds, including many of the founders, helping to establish common law in America. Contrary to Locke and to the founding fathers' views that were victorious in the *Radification Debates*, Blackstone argues in these *Commentaries* that government has "absolute despotic power," that government is an "absolute, uncontrolled authority," and "can do everything that is not naturally impossible." Blackstone rejected Locke's views on natural, moral law as "theoretical," that there are no such moral limitations on government. In Blackstone's view, government can do anything that is not specifically prohibited by its system of laws. Even Thomas Jefferson and James Wilson, two founding fathers, expressed concern over Blackstone's influence on law students and other political thinkers of the time and in the future.[28] In a letter written to James Madison in 1826, Jefferson makes reference to Blackstone's negative influence on pre-revolution, present and future law students. He says that Blackstone's influence had already turned New York and South Carolina away from the US Constitution,

> "In the selection of our Law Professor, we must be rigorously attentive to his political principles. You will recollect that before the revolution, Coke Littleton was the universal elementary book of law students, and a sounder whig never wrote, nor of profounder learning in the orthodox doctrines of the British constitution, or in what were called English liberties. You remember also that our lawyers were then all whigs. But when his black-letter text, and uncouth but cunning learning got out of fashion, and the honied Mansfieldism of Blackstone became the student's hornbook, from that moment, that profession (the nursery of our Congress) began to slide into toryism, and **nearly all the young brood of lawyers now are of that hue.** They suppose themselves, indeed, to be whigs, because they no longer know what whigism or republicanism means. It is in our seminary that that vestal flame is to be kept alive; it is thence it is to spread anew over our own and the sister States. If we are true and vigilant in our trust, within a dozen or twenty years a majority of our own legislature will be from one school, and many disciples will have carried its doctrines home with them to their several

States, and will have leavened thus the whole mass. New York has taken strong ground in vindication of the constitution; South Carolina had already done the same. Although I was against our leading, I am equally against omitting to follow in the same line, and backing them firmly; and I hope that yourself or some other will mark out the track to be pursued by us."[29] (bold added)

One of James Madison's appointed judges during his presidency, St. George Tucker, who was a law professor and who published an American version of Blackstone's *Commentaries,* said in the Appendix that Blackstone's view of government's unlimited sovereignty directly went against "the new lights which the American Revolution has spread over the science of politics." These "new lights" are *life, liberty* and *property.* Tucker was also very verbal in his sentiments against slavery and he articulated works in favor of emancipation, which ironically, at the time, went against adherents to Blackstonian theory.

During the early-mid 19th century, Blackstone's political philosophy began to and continues to directly influence law students and lawyers alike. Blackstone's views on absolute *statism* appealed to politicians and lawyers who defended slave owners, for example, and who likewise defended the institution of slavery in general.[30] Upon capture of a runaway slave, lawyers argued that the slave had to prove that he/she had the right to be free. Even James Madison had specifically argued earlier that contrary to Europe, in America, people are free, by their nature, that no person, absent conviction of a crime, should have to ask permission from government to be free.[31] Also,

Thomas Jefferson articulated that, "Under the law of nature, all men are born free," as a premise within *Samuel Howell v. Wade Netherland,* April 1770. Defiantly, Blackstone's views of liberty undermined, or many times even reversed Locke, Jefferson and Madison's views of freedom in the courts. Blackstone's view inspired and allowed lawyers, who also later became judges and politicians, as well as later influential political thinkers, to avoid the principles of natural, moral law, for the sake of *legal precedent,* and the restoration of absolute *statism* that dominated the English Monarchy. Blackstonian theory began structuring modern jurisprudence, thus later paving the way and underlying the "legal" arguments for Reconstruction policy and the Progressive Era. The Oath that is taken by government officials in the past and today, exemplifies the moral and political principles of Locke and of the founders. Yet, when a government official specifically adopts a view like Blackstone's, that is contrary to American principles, whereby their actions are divergent to securing the liberty and natural rights of the people, which includes property ownership, they should be deemed corrupt and a "domestic enemy."

This shift from America's foundational principles to such principles as Blackstone's can be seen creeping into case law since the Antebellum period within American history. Such arbitrary applications of government power have increased greatly, completely changing the way American government interprets fundamental rights, as well as property rights. Thus, over the last one hundred and fifty years or so, we have seen a digression from the founders' embodiment of Lock's political philosophy into Hobbesian and Blackstonian systems of government. And, today, this is still the fundamental question to ask, "What is the just and moral role of government?" The founding fathers say Locke's view is the best view of what the role of government is, and that view is what the Constitution is intended to secure. The neo-progressives and their likenesses in the courts say Blackstone's view is the best view of what the role of government should be. To oversimplify, we have, historically, two competing political *philosophies* working against each other within the American political landscape, and I don't mean democrat vs. republican. One is liberty based (Locke) and one is non-liberty based (Blackstone). Moreover, law enforcement today is predicated on the latter. The courts are riddled with the standards of Blackstonian theory, contrary to the foundational doctrine of property ownership found in Locke.

In *Sharpless vs. Philadelphia,* Blackstonian philosophy, which again is the belief that government can do whatever it wants that is not specifically restricted in its own system of laws, was a view held by the Pennsylvania Supreme Court Chief Justice Jeremiah Black. Black allowed government, in 1853, to invest taxpayer money in a private railroad. Justice Black wrote, "If the people of Pennsylvania had given all the authority which they themselves possessed, to a single person, they would have created a despotism as absolute in its control over life, liberty and property, as that of a Russian autocrat." Basically, through *implied consent,* rather than direct consent from the people in their representatives, the lawmakers, and likewise the courts, are only limited by their own judgments or discretions, unless law specifically prohibits same. This directly contradicts not only Locke, but also the founders' intent to limit lawmakers' ability to undermine property rights that are secured in the

Constitution. Ironically, this is how most people view American government actions today. This is why the spirit of the law must sync with the letter of the law. Blackstonian theory dominated the courts throughout the Progressive Era and into today. Again, this Blackstonian view is that government can do whatever it wants unless the Law specifically prohibits the act, and, that rights, including property rights, are created by society to serve and protect the interests of society itself, not the individual. Imagine how far you can run with this if you want to undo the Rule of Law. This is also why, in part, reinterpreting the Constitution as "practical" is so very important for neo-progressives. But, not practical in the sense you would think. Practical for government, not practical for the people. This rise of the philosophy of Pragmatism (practical), or Blackstonian Theory, has infected the American system of government like a virus, socially and intellectually engineering the people in government away from the vivacity and lawful adherence to their Oaths, which is designed to hold them accountable to both the wording and spirit of the Constitution. Timothy Sandefur, an adjunct scholar at the Cato Institute and attorney at the *Pacific Legal Foundation,* writes, as it relates to pragmatism,

> "Morality does not have any necessary connection to the nature of man, these intellectuals argued; rather, it is simply based on social agreement. Now that we had come to understand this fact, older moral and political beliefs – such as the sanctity of individual rights – could be altered in ways that would benefit society. The philosophy of pragmatism gave rise to the

Progressive Movement, a cultural and
political crusade that sought to liberate
society from what were once
considered timeless principles of right
and wrong, and to scientifically plan
the future of humanity."[32]

The legal system today is profoundly based in Blackstonian Theory, which helped give rise to the new *living document* interpretation of the US Constitution. In addition, the legal system today that is *enforced,* unbeknownst to most cops, arose from this collective, social and intellectual endeavor to restructure the American system of government from within the courts, in part, away from the fundamentals that created it, which are natural dispositions of right and wrong, and that human beings have fundamental rights that are *a priori* to society. It is rather satirical that neo-progressives really think, I mean they really believe that their pragmatic views of what America "should be," in likeness to European countries specifically, be primarily collectivist. And, they exploit law enforcement to make this world view as much a reality as possible.

This transition from Lockean to Blackstonian philosophy within case law can be best seen in *Nebbia vs. New York* (1934) where the US Supreme Court established the *Rational Basis Test,* which argues that *any* law is constitutional automatically, if said law is "rationally related to legitimate government interest." This then increases government's police powers over a person's property rights, arbitrarily. This also allows government to establish economic policy that promotes the "public welfare," wrote Justice Owen Roberts. He declared it constitutional that the New York law prevented people from selling milk at lower prices than other dairies, thus minimizing competition.[33] This *Rational Basis Test* directly undermines the *Due Process Clause* of the 4th, 5th and 14th Amendments, because it shifts the burden of proof onto the defendant when protecting their property rights from arbitrary legislation. Moreover, this new legal precedent, a pragmatic viewpoint, directly contradicts the Constitution and its mandated Rule of Law. Why? Because, adhering to the Rule of Law is *too difficult* for government officials who have grandiose ideas for social policy and progress. Thomas Jefferson warned William C. Jarvis, in a letter, of judicial despotism,

> "To consider the judges as the ultimate arbiters of all constitutional questions [is] a very dangerous doctrine indeed, and one which would place us under the despotism of an oligarchy. Our judges are as honest as other men and not more so. They have with others the same passions for party, for power, and the privilege of their corps. Their maxim is *boni judicis est ampliare jurisdictionem* [good justice is broad jurisdiction], and their power the more dangerous as they are in office for life and not responsible, as the other functionaries are, to the elective control. The Constitution has erected no such single tribunal, knowing that to whatever hands confided, with the corruptions of time and party, its members would become despots. It has more wisely made all the departments co-equal and co-sovereign within themselves."

Well how should the separation of powers constitutionally work? Jefferson continues,

> "The judges certainly have more frequent occasion to act on constitutional questions, because the laws of *meum* and *tuum* and of criminal action, forming the great mass of the system of law, constitute their particular department. When the legislative or executive functionaries act unconstitutionally, they are responsible to the people in their elective capacity. The exemption of the judges from that is quite dangerous enough... The people themselves,... [with] their discretion [informed] by education, [are] the true corrective of abuses of constitutional power."

As it relates to law enforcement, when a cop, for example, at any level of government, *impulsively* takes property from someone by force, like a cell phone, a gun, or land, even by warrant in many cases today, they are not only being exploited by the people who hold to this pragmatic ideology established in the courts, they are actualizing this Blackstonian, political philosophy into society that is directly opposed to the Constitution that they swore to uphold. The Constitution is still the Law of the Land. Therefore, the arguments for such pragmatic enforcement are unsound and are intended as "legal" usurpations. Hugh C. Murray, a California Supreme Court Justice rightly condemns Blackstonian, or pragmatic philosophy within legislation,

> "It has been erroneously supposed, by many, that the Legislature of a State

> might do any Act, except what was expressly prohibited by the Constitution....To serve the great end which that social compact was designed to secure, and, hence, it cannot be converted into such an unlimited power....Under our form of government, the legislature is not supreme...it can only exercise such powers as have been delegated to it, and when it steps beyond that boundary, its acts, like those of the most humble magistrate in the state who transcends his jurisdiction, are utterly void."[34]

When a State or the Federal government can create any law it wants simply because the State or Federal Constitution does not specifically prohibit such a law, and the cops then blindly enforce that law, *legislative tyranny* commences. The question to ask now is, how do we stop it? As mentioned before, progress within society is a very good thing. The founders progressively and successfully established personal liberty out of forced, monarchical collectivism. Part of this success came from the fact that genuine property ownership was secured in the Rule of Law as a means to secure individual liberty. To undermine property rights is to undermine liberty and the progression out of a monarchy. To use secondary laws to undermine the progress the founders fought for returns society into the history we progressed out of, where nobody truly owns property, not even their own bodies. The increase in population and the innovation of new technologies soundly and progressively give way to the necessary implementation of government legislation designed to secure and protect the rights of the people. Sanitation laws, new medicines oversight, for example, can enhance an individual's right to life. However, when the argument for progress shifts to undermining the fundamental rights of the people, like property ownership, as defined in the Declaration of Independence, the US Constitution and the State Ratification debates, then such liberty and property rights becomes a stumbling block for government, or rather for those individuals in government, who seek to instantiate a view opposite of the founders', like in the *Nebbia* case. Thus, it becomes imperative for neo-progressives in government to redefine rights, property and to redefine liberty. This is when secondary laws become arbitrary. I have yet to hear a sound argument, whereby modern technology or the legislative controls associated with population increases and/or behavior, can be a rational and justifiable means to rid Americans, in mass, of their fundamental right to own and be secure from poverty and government in their ownership of property. Collectivism, public safety, public policy, Blackstonian theory, Hobbesian and pragmatic philosophy, and the like, are not argument enough to emphasize and rationalize such legislative efforts as "progress." Neo-progressives have predicated this social progress on the necessary undermining of property rights, which began by the attempts to redefine what it means to own something. So to illustrate this irrational ideology, now that people have smart phones, for example, privacy must be sacrificed to protect their use of smart phones. Soon enough, even greater privacy will be scarified for the utilization of the US government's public biometric identification systems. It's coming.

Since the rise of the Progressive Era, true property ownership, and property rights in general, have dwindled greatly into more or less renting from a landlord, or near serfdom. The modern argument, propagated as evidence that you still "own" your property, is that you can "legally" possess and *resell* property. This is simple, social engineering. Recall, that absolute property ownership equals absolute control, and was established to secure free individuals from government intrusion and from extreme poverty, like homelessness. Like I've stated previously, it's not simply because of the government that people no longer truly own property, but because of certain people in government who hold a view of property contrary to our founding principles.

Redistribution of Wealth

Personal wealth is property, and its forced redistribution has its history in an array of philosophical ideas, like in *Marxism* or *Market Leninism,* for example. There are many sources for the idea of the *redistribution of wealth* to choose from, all in direct opposition of what America is really about, originally. Forced redistribution of wealth has always historically failed because of the corruption and greed attached to its implementation. History shows this. Human nature has not changed. Corruption creates the *economy of exclusion.* These philosophical dreams of economic utopia are implemented at the expense of the actual intended beneficiaries and the health of a sound financial culture, all in the name of fighting wealth inequality. When these grandiose ideas are implemented into free and open societies by force, it incites the need to intellectually and "legally" redefine initial and fundamental terms like *liberty, property,* and *rights,* at the expense of actual liberty, property and rights, because the actualization of the original terms are great hindrances to such grandiose ideas. Now new terms are created to actualize the redefining of the original terms, like *legal possession* and *registration,* as mentioned earlier. Recently, even Pope Frances said that the way to justifiably undermine the economy of exclusion is, "the legitimate redistribution of economic benefits by the state, as well as indispensable cooperation between the private sector and civil society."[35] This "legitimate redistribution of economic benefits by the state" is the source of financial inequality and the source of the *economy of exclusion* to begin with. Moreover, the forced redistribution of wealth actually creates more poverty because the corrupt and greedy people, who hold the power of oversight, dip their fingers into the pie, somehow, someway. Redistribution of wealth by forcefully extracting wealth from other people is not the answer because not only is it immoral, it is stealing. If an action is wrong, it's wrong. America is a nation built upon natural law and the genuine equality of all people, remember? Government people cannot steal from non-government people ethically. But they do, they do it by socially engineering cops to believe it's the law, and that it's for the good of the people. Retired Philadelphia Police Captain Ray Lewis said in a televised interview recently, of law enforcement, that, "It's an oppressive organization now controlled by the one percent of corporate America. Corporate America is using police forces as their mercenaries." This statement is the essence of what this book is about.

The financial world today is unbelievably complicated because the original terms aforementioned, which are the underpinning of the country, are not upheld and enforced anymore. Why? Because humans in government want to control humans not in government, which includes all of their personal and business finances, as a means to curb the probability that individuals or businesses may commit a financial crime, or not be successful. That is *theoretical* politics in action. Secondary laws designed on the probability of criminal activity are virtually always against the Constitution. So, what happens if the state self-referentially applies its own logic? Exactly, it fails. It fails because human nature is still the dominant, negative force in government. Today and in the past, greed in government, for example, can be when a judge seeks to attach their name to precedent. Greed can be when the legislator seeks to attach their name to a piece of legislation. Greed can be when the cop seeks to execute their will simply because they are a cop. All these arbitrary attributes of greed within government are the direct result of the individuals ignorantly nullifying their oath and forgetting who their *dutiful* maker is, the US Constitution. Yes, a document. Recall that is was a document, the Magna Carta, that initially undermined the absolute sovereign power of Kings.

The original financial system is a free and open market founded upon capitalist principles. Sound Law is in place to go after those who commit financial crimes or financial fraud. Within this sound financial system, forced redistribution of wealth cannot exist, just as forced fairness cannot exist in our original Constitutional Republic. Silent encroachments must take place first. The rebuttal against this original capitalist system goes like this; technology and the increase in financial diversification within the financial system today, coupled with increases in population, demand more intrusive regulations, at the expense of financial privacy, for the well being of society as a whole. Regulations can be a necessary and good thing. Yet, greed and the security of special interest income create intrusive regulations, as its own source of revenue, thus creating a completely different financial system that excludes the non-wealthy, and thus extracts wealth from the people in mass, all by force. This works when the legislators criminalize any and all financial innovations related to free market principles, at the whim of appeasing special interests, simply on the probability of coming in second to the wealth of the people. This also happens when any and everything has a price, especially those things necessary to simply exist. A recent study done at Princeton and Northwestern University has declared that America is no longer a democracy, nor a republic, that

America is an actual *oligarchy*, run by a powerful elite.[35.5]

Senator Bernie Sanders touched upon this by asking the Federal Reserve Chair Janet Yellen, "Are we still a capitalist democracy or have we gone over into an oligarchic form of society in which incredible economic and political power now rests with the billionaire class?"[36] Yellen responded and admitted that she no longer knows what type of financial system America has, "I don't know what to call our system....I prefer not to give labels, but there's no question we've had the trend toward growing inequality, and I personally find it a very worrisome trend that deserves the attention of policy makers."[37] The most intrusive and ultimately destructive aspect of the forced redistribution of wealth, furthermore, is designed to undermine genuine property ownership in the name of "wealth equality," which is actually moving backwards and is blatantly counter-constitutional. The question to ask is, is the contemporary process of the redistribution of wealth actually making average Americans poorer?

The Russell Sage Foundation published an economic study in the summer of 2014 entitled *Wealth Levels, Wealth Inequality, and the Great Recession,* showing that the typical household in 2003 held a net-worth of about $87,992. In 2013, the typical household held a net- worth of only about $56,335. That is a drop of nearly thirty-six percent. This was, in part, due to the housing bubble, and the Great Recession. There is something deeper that is causing inflation and the drop of household wealth. Fabian T. Pfeffer, the University of Michigan professor who led the study said, "The housing bubble basically hid a trend of declining financial wealth at the median that began in 2001."[37.5] What hidden trend?

The study concluded,

> "While large absolute amounts of wealth were destroyed at the top of the wealth distribution, households at the bottom of the wealth distribution lost the largest share of their total wealth. As a result, wealth inequality increased significantly from 2003 through 2013. The American economy has experienced rising income and wealth inequality for several decades, and there is little evidence that these trends are likely to reverse in the near term. It is possible that the very slow recovery from the Great Recession will continue to generate increased wealth inequality in the coming years as those hardest hit may still be drawing down the few assets they have left to cover current consumption and the housing market continues to grow at a modest pace."

Wealth redistribution has always been an *unsound* and an unethical process within an oligarchy because financial elitists run it at the expense of the wealth of society as a whole. And, they do it in the name of the "common good." Displacement of blame within such a financial system is always pointed away from the actual system itself, covertly, which is the real source of wealth inequality. Such a stealthy government financial system is based upon many controversial and necessary factors: debt based currency, any and everything having a price, an easily manipulable monetary policy, non-allodial or non-absolute ownership of real property by private individuals, property and financial laws designed to maximize government and corporate interests, tricky "legal" trading practices within the stock market, devaluation of the dollar through inflation, the conversion of property and financial rights into privileges, credit based government spending while forcing a tax on labor to pay the interest on such use of credit, government pensions funded by future generations, forced economic activity, and the list goes on. What did President Franklin D. Roosevelt mean when he wrote in a private letter to Colonel Edward House in 1933 that, "a financial element in the large centers has owned the government ever since the days of Andrew Jackson?" What did Vice President John Calhoun mean when he said in a speech in 1836 that, "A power has risen up in the government greater than the people themselves, consisting of many and various powerful interests, combined in one mass, and held together by the cohesive power of the vast surplus in banks?" What did President Woodrow Wilson mean when he wrote in 1913, after signing the Federal Reserve Act and the Income Tax Amendment, that,

> "A great industrial nation is controlled by its system of credit. Our system of credit is privately concentrated. The growth of the nation, therefore, and all our activities are in the hands of a few men...[W]e have come to be one of the worst ruled, one of the most completely controlled and dominated, governments in the civilized world - no longer a government by free opinion, no longer a government by conviction and the vote of the majority, but a government by the opinion and the duress of small groups of dominant men. Since I entered politics, I have chiefly had men's views confided to me privately. Some of the biggest men in the United States, in the

field of commerce and manufacture, are afraid of something. They know that there is a power somewhere so organized, so subtle, so watchful, so interlocked, so complete, so pervasive, that they had better not speak above their breath when they speak in condemnation of it?"

What did Congressman Louis T. McFadden mean when he said in a speech to Congress in 1932,

"Mr. Chairman, we have in this country one of the most corrupt institutions the world has ever known. I refer to the Federal Reserve Board and the Federal Reserve Banks. The Federal Reserve Board, a Government board, has cheated the Government of the United States and the people of the United States out of enough money to pay the national debt. Mr. Chairman, when the Federal Reserve act was passed, the people of the United States did not perceive that a world system was being set up here...and that this country was to supply financial power to an international super-state, a super-state controlled by international bankers and international industrialists acting together to enslave the world for their own pleasure?"

What did Senator William Jenner mean when he said in a 1954 speech that,

"Today the path to total dictatorship in the U.S. can be laid by strictly legal means... We have a well-organized political-action group in this country, determined to destroy our Constitution and establish a one-party state...It operates secretly, silently, continuously to transform our Government... This ruthless power-seeking elite is a disease of our century... This group... is answerable neither to the President, the Congress, nor the courts. It is practically irremovable?"

What did New York City Mayor John F. Hylan mean in 1922 when he said in the NY Times that,

"The real menace of our Republic is the invisible government, which like a giant octopus sprawls its slimy legs over our cities, states and nation... The little coterie of powerful international bankers virtually run the United States government for their own selfish purposes. They practically control both parties... and control the majority of the newspapers and magazines in this country. They use the columns of these papers to club into submission or drive out of office public officials who refuse to do the bidding of the powerful corrupt cliques which compose the invisible government. It operates under cover of a self- created screen [and] seizes our executive officers, legislative bodies, schools, courts, newspapers and every agency created for the public protection?"

What did J. Edgar Hoover mean when he wrote in the Elks Magazine in 1956 that, "The individual is handicapped by coming face-to-face with a conspiracy so monstrous he cannot believe it exists. The American mind simply has not come to a realization of the evil which has been introduced into our midst. It rejects even the assumption that human creatures could espouse a philosophy which must ultimately destroy all that is good and decent?" This financial system, this oligarchy, has become the norm in America. Moreover, the sustaining of this financial system is also the foundation of law enforcement. Such an oligarchic system can't work without force, or at the least the exploitation of force, especially in light of our republic's foundational principles being fundamentally contrary.

During the mid 19th Century, a new philosophy arose in North America that directly affected genuine property ownership and the rise of this oligarchy within the United States; the *Georgist Philosophy,* or *Georgism.* Contrary to the founders' emphasis on absolute ownership of property within the realm of necessary existence, or property that was essentially basic, which included land, a home and tools of the trade, Henry George (1839-1897), an economist and philosopher, whole-heartedly in his own mind, developed a philosophy intended to minimize poverty and a means for all people to acquire *legal possession* of property through the *Land Value Tax,* a property tax. Recall that it was originally William The Conqueror in the 11th Century who redivided up the land into shires, established an additional tax on land and property (quit-rent) and then appointed a *Shire-Reeve* (Sheriff) to collect those taxes by force, all as a means to increase the wealth and power of the new King, essentially ending true ownership of a home by the people in England, all through violence and theft. The founders specifically worked against this, as we touched on earlier. Many people in 19th Century American government liked this ideology, however, because it increased the wealth and power of the local governments. The problem with this political philosophy is, that it not only directly flies into the face of Locke, the American Revolution, the Constitution and individual liberty, it has easily been *taken for granted,* thus allowing the legal system to slippery slope into the forced taxation of virtually all property having any taxable value whatsoever, outside of the actual contents of a home. And, being that rights derive from property, when property rights are thwarted by way of a tax, so are all rights. This is another example of Blackstonian theory, which allows the government to do what it wants as long as what it wants is not directly prohibited within its system of laws. In addition, this redefining of property ownership creates forced *co-ownership* of property between government as principal owner and the citizen as co-owner, or legal possessor. Government, again, is a mere entity, only made up of other people and cannot actually own anything. Therefore, it is the other people in government, collectively, who by the monopoly of force, come to own and control the use of an individual's property, not "society." Such a pro-collectivist statement, as it relates to the state owning property, is nonsense. Moreover, and most intrusively, this forced redistribution of property, directly *secures* a "legal" path for local, state and federal government officials to intimately dive into the private and personal life of the individual, through the barrel of a cop's gun. What about the security of the individual from poverty or from government intrusion, as the intended purpose of property rights? Just recently the Bureau of Labor Statistics for May of 2014 reported that the poorest American families spend upwards to forty percent of their income on housing alone.38 Can we actually restore financial equality, or at minimum, secure people against the most devastating effects of being poor, which is hunger and homelessness?

Georgist philosophy is one intentionally developed to redistribute wealth, George says that, "What has destroyed every previous civilization has been the tendency to the unequal distribution of wealth and power."39 Yes, this is true, which is why, in part, the founders acknowledged the need to secure individual property ownership, opposite of "previous civilizations," by establishing absolute or true ownership of the very basics, like a plot of land and a home. Redistribution of wealth today, as originating in Georgism, has actually deviated open societies back into the likeness of "previous civilizations" by legally thwarting true property ownership through this land value tax, allowing government to become richer and more powerful, as William The Conqueror intended. In many countries, for example, some governments actually tax the value of property *inside* a family's home, like Germany. Local governments have tried this in America, but the 4th Amendment stops them, thankfully. In "previous civilizations," extracting wealth from the populace always funded and secured the aristocracy's separation from commoners, who were deemed unequal. The destruction of governments in the past was of moral consequences, masked as pure economic issues, as will happen here. Recall, that the American founders ended the immoral practices of feudalism and serfdom, or theft. Henry George comes along and resurrects both; because, people are again, as in feudalism, forced to work as a means to pay *quit-rent* to government in order to simply live on the land they think they "own".

Again, Georgism sounds nice, but Georgism is the history of the world, as it relates to property rights, repeating itself.

A recent article on WashingtonsBlog.com, written by Charles Smith, touched upon how not only neo-progressives control property through credit creation, manipulation, and the "reduction of selfhood," but that the process is a *new style* of feudalism in America, also know as neo-feudalism. Smith describes neo-feudalism as necessarily dependant upon neo-progressives, "those with access to the low-interest unlimited credit spigot of the Federal Reserve become more equal than others – the perfect Orwellian description of a Neofeudal arrangement in which financial leverage buys not just rentier assets but political power and control." Thus, to summarize the endgame of neo-feudalism, Smith cites correspondent Bart D,

> "What if financial elites enter the market with their 'free' Federal Reserve cash and buy up a lions' share of accommodation to keep home ownership unaffordable and force the majority to live as renters? If, in a dwindling economy, the Power Elite can't hold power over the masses by keeping their jobs or other income streams under threat, maybe they will switch to wanting everyone to owe them rent and use the threat of homelessness as another tool to keep people under control. It's an extension of the food stamps concept. The system is moving towards making sure most people don't have future access to the resources that enable them to survive and create wealth

outside of the system. I think the economy is now about controlling people. We are headed for a societal structure in which opportunities to rise economically will be increasingly stifled by those at the top. The money is irrelevant now, the real game is being played is in controlling tangible and 'essential for life' assets: housing, water delivery, food, clothing, energy. Those at the top want power to control everyone below them, particularly to keep them from revolting."[40]

Even NASA suggested that societies have collapsed in the past because it did not redistribute wealth.[41] I see this as a bit over simplistic and ironic. Past societies collapsed because of corruption, the greed for power, and the forced extraction of wealth from the masses. Governments failed by not creating a path of equal opportunity for all people to acquire wealth and to keep it. In addition, past governments failed by not securing a way to own property in absolute, as the founders originally did for Americans. The past arguments for such inequality has been a collectivist effort, evidenced in the extraction of more wealth from all people by way of quit-rent. Quit-rent, especially from one's own income, in and of itself, is still forced collectivism through the exploitation of law enforcement. This is the direct result of American government becoming more business oriented rather than liberty oriented. Individualism and absolute property ownership are what real progression out of history is, because, it secures the individual from poverty by allowing them to have a place to live, which is a basic necessity of existence, and they can think for themselves, absent the threat of death by the state. Failed governments happen because of the want of more power. Modern governments set themselves up for future failure by creating fiat currencies, as a means to get around the finiteness of real money. Thus, modern governments rely upon borrowing at the expense of the people's labor and the future labor of the unborn, creating massive debt that future generations must pay by force. This is grossly unethical. This is what will primarily lead to the fall of a nation today, the failure of fiat currency. Not the lack of redistributing wealth, but the failure of allowing people to keep their wealth, which is their property. Governments would not have to borrow as much at the expense of future generations to help secure the poor from being poorer if the people were allowed to own their basic property in allodium, as intended.

Stanley Druckenmiller, a hedge fund manager and philanthropist, recently said of the Federal Reserve's continued *quantitative easing* and its decision to delay the tightening of monetary policy, "This is fantastic for every rich person... this is the biggest redistribution of wealth from the middle class and the poor to the rich ever."[42] *Redistributing wealth* is more of a modern *tongue in cheek* move for governments in bed with corporate interests to amass more wealth for themselves and power, while appearing to appeal to set standards of benevolence. When an individual must spend all their time acquiring income to be forcefully *redistributed* and to forcefully pay taxes on property they only legally possess, such private charity efforts become impractical because the average person has virtually no income left, thus the need arises for government to forcefully extract more wealth and to borrow more currency to turn around and subsidize those very people. It is a vicious circle that ends horribly. The end result of bad government economic policy and the forced transfer of wealth is *income inequality.* Nobel economist Joseph Stiglitz said,

> "Inequality is not inevitable. It is not ... like the weather, something that just happens to us. It is not the result of the laws of nature or the laws of economics. Rather, it is something that we create, by our policies, by what we do.... We created this inequality—chose it, really—with [bad] laws ..."[43]

Stiglitz also said that the government's toxic asset plan, a scheme to inflate the value of assets held by banks, basically "amounts to robbery of the American people". Economics professor Randall Wray writes, "Thieves...took over the whole economy and the political system lock, stock, and barrel. They didn't just blow up finance, they oversaw the swiftest transfer of wealth to the very top the world has ever seen."[44] In this same spirit, highly regarded economist Michael Hudson, Distinguished Research Professor at the University of Missouri, Kansas City, said,

> "You have to realize that what they're trying to do is to roll back the Enlightenment, roll back the moral philosophy and social values of classical political economy and its culmination in Progressive Era legislation, as well as the New Deal institutions. They're not trying to make the economy more equal, and they're not trying to share power. Their greed is (as Aristotle noted) infinite. So what you find to be a violation of traditional values is a re-assertion of pre-industrial, **feudal values.** The economy is being set back on the road to debt

peonage. The Road to Serfdom is not government sponsorship of economic progress and rising living standards, it's the dismantling of government, the dissolution of regulatory agencies, to create a new feudal-type elite."[45] (bold added)

Harry Dent, of Dent Research, an economic think tank that predicts economic waves, stated that the U.S. and Europe are headed in the same direction as Japan, a country still in a "coma economy precisely because it never let its debt bubble deleverage." Dent argues, "The only way we will not follow in Japan's footsteps is if the Federal Reserve stops printing new money."[46]

Like I've mentioned earlier, society, as it relates to human nature, is actually digressing back into history, and history tells all, or at least most. Government's intent to force fairness and redistribute wealth by controlling and owning property is actually leading all of us back into a soft, feudal type of culture. This can be stopped in America when and if people truly own their essentially basic property, as intended by our founders. Many neo-progressives will come along and reinterpret the founders into a contemporary view that says no such arrangement had been established at the founding, as it relates to absolute property ownership. This is completely in effort to maintain the status quo. Study it out for yourself. We all know that most tax revenue created to fund social programs goes directly to the bureaucracy and enforcement attached to its implementation. The neo-progressives also argue that private charities would not be enough to sustain the amount of help people need. In other words, private charities are not enough to also fund the government's control of property and to secure its financial incentive.

On the other hand, I also want to assert the genuine and necessary balance of progress in American society that also entails economic compromise within the social contract. Such economic compromise does allow limited property taxation, or redistribution of property to benefit the collective, which does include helping the poor and to fund some social programs designed to temporarily help people who may need it. This is a good thing and most Americans support these sound progressive policies founded in reasonable taxation. The founders understood this, yet tried to minimize its abuses through the balance of property rights and limited taxation of property. John Locke says that,

> "Every one, as he is bound to preserve himself, and not to quit his station wilfully, so by the like reason, when his own preservation comes not in competition, ought he, as much as he can, to preserve the rest of mankind, and may not, unless it be to do justice on an offender, take away, or impair the life, or what tends to the preservation of the life, the liberty, health, limb, or goods of another."[47]

Society as a whole has a duty to care for the handicapped, or indigent, for example. But the *forced* redistribution of wealth at the expense of basic property rights and the basic necessities of life is unethical, because it actually creates poverty. How is attaching monetary value to the basic necessities of human existence, like water, food, land, tools to cultivate land, a home, any more ethical than a woman attaching monetary value to her own vagina? Such efforts of government to capitalize on the essentials of human existence for profit, through bedding down with corporations and special interests, are unethical and are neo-progressive, because they adhere to a political philosophy that accentuates the power of government rather than the genuine, natural property rights of free individuals. This is pragmatism at work. Why not capitalize on air then? Oh wait, the Carbon Tax. I am not referring to essentials like water, food, a home and land that are valued beyond what is necessary to exist. The social contract employs compromise, not dominance. Yet crony-capitalism dominates. Maybe if income tax revenue were rechanneled into securing the basic property ownership for people rather than funding an empire abroad, poverty would be a lot less a social problem in America. Actually poverty is a money problem. If the homeless, for example, were spending money, then there would probably be *homeless special interest groups,* with bureaucracy attached. But since homelessness is not about actual homelessness, local governments make it illegal to feed the homeless because they don't actually buy the food. Pacifying human hunger now takes a back seat to liability. The neo-progressive sentiment is, that homelessness is not good for business. The National Law Center on Homelessness and Poverty, and MSNBC, reported in July 2014, that about 187 cities across America are banning homelessness, which, "prohibit sleeping in public, begging in public, loitering, sitting or lying down in public spaces, food sharing, and sleeping in vehicles, among other behaviors." The report states that, "Many cities have chosen to criminally punish people living on the street for doing what any human being must do to survive." The report further asserts, "Despite a lack of any available alternatives, more cities are choosing to turn the necessary conduct of homeless people into criminal activity.... Such laws threaten the human and constitutional rights of homeless people, impose unnecessary costs on cities, and do nothing to solve the problems they purport to address."[47.5] So, when a cop arrests someone for feeding a homeless person, is the cop doing his or her job ethically? Are they upholding the rule of law or are they upholding an elitist agenda? There is a relatively simple alternative that puts a significant dent into poverty and homelessness. The founders came up with such a solution. But like I also mentioned earlier, the founder' solutions for poverty and homelessness are, sadly for oligarchs, not good for America as a business model. Because, its all really about money, or currency actually, and homeless people not having a *strawman*.

Neo-progressive policy increases the power of government for its own sake, and, it surrenders by force the privacy and property of the individual to the bureaucratic endeavor of *forced charity* in the name of helping the poor. Even Benjamin Franklin acknowledged, "In different countries...the more public provisions were made for the poor, the less they provided for themselves, and of course became poorer. And, on the contrary, the less was done for them, the more they did for themselves, and became richer."[48] The proper role of government is to secure the citizen's capability, with very little help from the government, to take care of themselves first and then the poor, to the best of their financial ability. There must be a balance that secures government revenue and secures people from poverty, absent a welfare state. Sound poise is not the case today, however. Most peace loving people don't have a problem with limited property taxation to fund social programs, to help pay for police and fire, or to help secure services that care for those who cannot otherwise care for themselves. This is a good thing, and again, a sound aspect of Locke's social contract coupled with the founders' limited role of government. Even George Washington emphasized *proportion* in a letter to Alexander Hamilton in 1783, "It may be laid down, as a primary position, and the basis of our system, that every citizen who enjoys the protection of a free government, owes not only a proportion of his property, but even of his personal services to the defense of it..." Fundamentally, it takes most of us, some through defensive capabilities, and a proportion of our property, or a property tax, and other avenues of reasonable taxation to help keep the peace. Today, a proportion of the value of all property, which is the land, the house and all other property outside the home, like a car, a boat, a trailer, etc. are all taxed, which is a corruption of what the founders had in mind, but more consistent with Georgism. Taxing the value of basic and essential property does not secure one from poverty, nor from government intrusion, as intended, thus Georgism prevails because such taxation is intended to secure government revenue first.

So how can American governments, today, put a significant dent into poverty and homelessness? A sound taxation scheme on private and real property should only be applied beyond a certain valuation, securing the basic necessities that it takes to live freely and securely. Today, the federal government, county governments, state governments, municipal governments and the like, tax any and all property of any value whatsoever, including income. Ben Franklin commented on a sound principle for taxing property in a letter,

> "All the Property that is necessary to a Man, for the Conservation of the Individual and the Propagation of the Species, is his natural Right, which none can justly deprive him of: **But all Property superfluous to such purposes is the Property of the Publick, who, by their Laws, have created it, and who may therefore by other Laws dispose of it, whenever the Welfare of the Publick shall demand such Disposition.** He that does not like civil Society on these Terms, let him retire and live among Savages. He can have no right to the benefits of Society, who will not pay his Club towards the Support of it."[49] (bold added)

It would make more economic and *lawful* sense today, to concur with Franklin, that non-commercial, real property, for example, is only taxed above a certain value, which secures lower income people on their land and in their homes. Even in their tools of their trade, like a tractor. Taxes would only be extracted from property that was not essential to existence, or as Franklin says, taxes should only apply to property that is *superfluous,* or beyond essential. A small plot of land to cultivate and a home to live in and raise a family are essentially basic to existence and should not be taxed. This is actually backed up by the Supreme Court of Tenn. in *Corn v. Fort*, 1936, "...the individual's Right to live and own property are natural rights for the enjoyment of which an excise cannot be imposed." "An excise" means a tax. This is what the founders argued for. This would not only better secure general equality between all people, it would also secure natural rights. Most importantly, the non-taxation of essentially basic, real property, secures those who have less from homelessness. Because, as Franklin says, "All the Property that is necessary to a Man, for the Conservation of the Individual and the Propagation of the Species, is his natural Right, which **none can justly deprive him of.**" Thus, taxation of all property at any valuation, like a family's basic necessity of a home and land to grow food, or their basic income, is "unjustly" depriving the individual of their natural right, which is exactly what Georgism advocates.

Thomas Jefferson also asserted this very same thing; that property tax should only apply to property above a certain value, as a way to sustain genuine equality, and to protect people from deviating into extreme poverty and homelessness. Such property laws are a sound protection of one's natural property rights. Property laws that allow no limitation on property tax below a certain value violate the natural rights of property ownership. Thus Jefferson writes to James Madison,

> "But after all these comes the most numerous of all the classes, that is, the poor who cannot find work. I asked myself what could be the reason that so many should be permitted to beg who are willing to work, in a country where there is a very considerable proportion of uncultivated lands? These lands are kept idle mostly for the aske of game. It should seem then that it must be because of the enormous wealth of the proprietors which places them above attention to the increase of their revenues by permitting these lands to be laboured. I am conscious that an equal

division of property is impracticable. But the consequences of this enormous inequality producing so much misery to the bulk of mankind, legislators cannot invent too many devices for subdividing property, only taking care to let their subdivisions go hand in hand with the natural affections of the human mind. The descent of property of every kind therefore to all the children, or to all the brothers and sisters, or other relations in equal degree is a politic measure, and a practicable one. Another means of silently lessening the inequality of property **is to exempt all from taxation below a certain point,** and to tax the higher portions of property in geometrical progression as they rise. Whenever there is in any country, uncultivated lands and unemployed poor, it is clear that the laws of property have been so far extended as to violate natural right. The earth is given as a common stock for man to labour and live on. If, for the encouragement of industry we allow it to be appropriated, we must take care that other employment be furnished to those excluded from the appropriation.[50] (bold added)

Property taxes on any and all property of value, especially on private land and houses, and on any and all income, today, are secured through property law because the intent of such laws are *business oriented* to sustain special interests and government power, rather than being liberty oriented, which limits power, as Jefferson notes. Recall that the income tax was intended for the top one percent of income earners, not for poor people who had very little income. But now virtually all people are taxed at all levels of income, "from whatever source derived," as mandated in the 16th Amendment. *Internal Revenue* has become the federal government's primary source of wealth, as opposed to external revenue, as the founders intended.

In fact, Jefferson and Madison were against the Federal government having permanent, internal revenue that derives from the people, at all. Madison, in response to the first Act to raise revenue from within the country, which was signed by Washington, said that, "...a national revenue must be obtained; but the system must be such a one, that, while it secures the object of revenue it shall not be oppressive to our constituents."[50.5] The Act did not impose taxes on the people in mass whatsoever, but only on merchandise imported by *mercantile citizens*. The founders believed that internal revenue, if necessary, must be temporary only, as in a time of war, for example. Jefferson and Madison articulated that the federal government's primary source of revenue must only derive from "external duties," from foreigners who seek the privilege of doing business in America. Jefferson points this out in his second Inaugural address in 1805,

> "At home, fellow citizens, you best know whether we have done well or ill. The suppression of unnecessary offices, of useless establishments and expenses, enabled us to discontinue our internal taxes.... The remaining revenue on the consumption of foreign articles, is paid cheerfully by those who can afford to add foreign luxuries to domestic

comforts, being collected on our seaboards and frontiers only, and incorporated with the transactions of our mercantile citizens, it may be the pleasure and pride of an American to ask, what farmer, what mechanic, what laborer, ever sees a tax-gatherer of the United States?" (Bold Added)

In a nutshell, as the Executive Branch grew in power over time through the creation of regulatory agencies and their attached bureaucracies, the Federal Government could no longer financially sustain its power through external sources, as the founders intended, so America began to feed upon itself, it turned inward for revenue, to feed on the American people's labor and property. Moreover, as it relates to taxation for redistribution, Jefferson is clear on misinterpreting the General Welfare Clause for this purpose. Jefferson asserts in a letter to Joseph Milligan, April 6, 1816 (On political economy) that, "To take from one, because it is thought his own industry and that of his father has acquired too much, in order to spare to others who (or whose fathers) have not exercised equal industry and skill, is to violate arbitrarily the first principle of association, 'to guarantee to everyone a free exercise of his industry and the fruits acquired by it.'" In the end, as a means to secure internal revenue anyway, in spite of the fact that it was grossly frowned upon by the founders as oppressive, isn't it nice how the government simply amended the Constitution to empower itself financially, completely contrary to the spirit of it?

The natural rights to own basic, non-luxury property, to secure one's basic existence from homelessness and extreme poverty, is violated when one must, by force, pay a government a tax to exercise owning that property. Imagine how such a limited tax valuation policy would help the poor. The option to acquire Allodial Title (absolute ownership) on non-commercial, privately owned, real property, under a certain value, when a mortgage is paid in full, is sound property law. This also frees one up to pursue further passions and ambitions without worrying about the need to constantly come up with payments to simply live in their home that they have spent years paying a bank for. They are secure in the "Property that is necessary to a Man, for the Conservation of the Individual and the Propagation of the Species," as Ben Franklin asserted. They don't ever have to worry about becoming homeless in their lifetime. In addition, owning property in allodium allows room for younger people to work the jobs that older people must work in order to pay rent/tax to local governments to stay in their homes after retirement. Yet, contrary to sound compromise, it is the basic and essential property that modern government bureaucracy arbitrarily thrives upon, which works directly against what Franklin, Jefferson and Washington emphasized above. We all know what happens when this sort of *tax-all* is created and enforced. Most goes to government itself, which ultimately inflates the currency and, again, also increases the intrusion of government into the private life of the individual, because it wants more. It then also increases the debt, whereby the government must dream up more ways to tax property and extract wealth, to pay the interest on that debt and to fund more bureaucracy and its enforcement. This is not what the founders had in mind.

If I were a state or even a federal representative who, to the best of my ability, tried to adhere to the founders' view on property, I would author a Bill at the state level that limited taxation on the people's non-commercial, essentially basic, real property, to a certain valuation, consistent with the fluctuation of the cost of living and inflation. I would also establsh an allodial title application process on real property that was essentially basic and absent leins. At the federal level, I would seek to limit the income tax to only a certain amount of income by either statute or by actually amending the 16th Amendment. So hypothetically, the federal government could not tax income under $30k per year per individual. Or, for example, local governments could not tax real property, a house and land, under a $200k value per year per family or individual, depending on the location and corresponding valuation to such a mandate. This is what helps the poor, not redistribution of wealth. The neo-progressives would cry out that this is not fair. No, what is not fair are tax breaks for the rich that prevent actual fairness. Oh my, can you also imagine the corporate lobbyists, lawyers, special interest groups, banks, and the like, that would target my office and other possible sponsors of my Bill? All parties would be hell-bent to kill such a Bill, because actually securing property rights is not in the best interest of government as a *business*. Even if such a Bill were to become law, the Bill would be manipulated by amendments, as a means to maximize tax revenue for private pockets. One-roomed cabins would become palaces on paper, for example.

In 1794, when the 3rd Congress appropriated $15,000 to assist some French refugees, James Madison, in a speech, objected to this redistribution of wealth by saying, "I cannot undertake to lay my finger on that article of the Constitution which granted a right to Congress of expending, on objects of benevolence, the money of their constituents." However, Madison was not necessarily against monies allocated to help the poor, or the French in this case. He was afraid of such allocation of funds establishing a dangerous precedent. The *Annals of Congress,* therefore, put his point into context:

> "Mr. Madison wished to relieve the sufferers, but was afraid of establishing a dangerous precedent, which might hereafter be perverted to the countenance of purposes very different from those of charity. He acknowledged, for his own part, that he could not undertake to lay his finger on that article in the Federal Constitution which granted a right of Congress of expending, on objects of benevolence, the money of their constituents."

The redistribution of wealth is not the same thing as helping the poor. Government officials get no moral credit for helping the poor through the barrel of a gun. Forced charity has created bad precedent that has paved the road to redistribution. Madison later added, "The government of the United States is a definite government, confined to specified objects. It is not like the state governments, whose powers are more general. Charity is no part of the legislative duty of this government."[51] Legislative duty refers to *sound* precedent. The irony is, that neo- progressives will argue that this ideology of Madison's is outdated. The US Constitution is still the Law of the Land because human nature has not changed, only technology and knowledge have increased. In addition, the present abuse of the *welfare state* in America has grown to become unsustainable and unbelievably costly because the federal and state governments have, contrary to Madison's and the other founders' views, like Franklin and Jefferson, made charity a monstrous part of the "legislative duty" of government, by force. Since America is now a corporation under Title 28 of the US Code, whereby everything under the sun has a price, the welfare state has become a means to keep the poor *economically active,* to keep them spending. This is the purpose of the redistribution of wealth. It is now impossible to go back. To financially trim, significantly, the welfare state today would create panic and chaos in the streets, because, for statism, state dependency has become a paramount incentive to social engineering and control, which leads to the need to monopolize force, to keep it working as smoothly as possible. A reasonable question to ask now is, would there be such a concept as *illegal immigration* had the American welfare state not gotten out of control? Another question to ask is, how did this all begin? I want to cite, in part, an elitist document published by William Cooper in his book *Behold A Pale Horse.* Cooper, a former Navy Intelligence Officer, advises that the document is a *top-secret* programming/technical manual for acquiring mass control over property, social and economic activity. The title of the document is called, *Silent Weapons for Quiet Wars.* Cooper also articulates that this neo-progressive agenda was written and set in motion during the mid fifties, whereby aristocracy must replace genuine American equality,

> "Consequently, in the interest of future world order, peace, and tranquility, it was decided to privately wage a quiet war against the American public with an

ultimate objective of permanently shifting the natural and social energy (wealth) of the undisciplined and irresponsible many into the hands of the self-disciplined, responsible, and worthy few.... In order to achieve a totally predictable economy, the low-class elements of society must be brought under total control, i.e., must be housebroken, trained, and assigned a **yoke** and long-term social duties from a very early age, before they have an opportunity to question the propriety of the matter. In order to achieve such conformity, the lower- class family unit must be disintegrated by a process of increasing preoccupation of the parents and the establishment of government-operated day-care centers for the occupationally orphaned children. The quality of education given to the lower class must be of the poorest sort, so that the moat of ignorance isolating the inferior class from the superior class is and remains incomprehensible to the inferior class. With such an initial handicap, even bright lower class individuals have little if any hope of extricating themselves from their assigned lot in life. This form of slavery is essential to maintain some measure of social order, peace, and tranquility for the ruling upper class." (bold added)

This agenda is, in part, the underpinning of the modern legal system. As it relates to welfare again, Cooper also cites from *Silent Wars* that,

> "The social welfare program is nothing
> more than an open-ended credit balance
> system which creates a false capital
> industry to give nonproductive people a
> roof over their heads and food in their
> stomachs. This can be useful, however,
> because the recipients become state
> property in return for the "gift," a
> standing army for the elite. For he who
> pays the piper picks the tune. Those who
> get hooked on the economic drug, must
> go to the elite for a fix. In this, the
> method of introducing large amounts of
> stabilizing capacitance is by borrowing
> on the future "credit" of the world."

Now ask, what might the "yoke" be that this document is referring to? "In this structure, credit, presented as a pure element called 'currency,' has the appearance of capital, but is in effect negative capital. Hence, it has the appearance of service, but is in fact, indebtedness or debt."[51.2]

Another example of this compulsory redistribution of wealth is the forced *registration* of property, like with a vehicle, for example. Around 2005-06 I was a bit shaken by some information I had read in Michael Badnarik's book: *Good to be King.* He had talked about how the title to a vehicle was not the actual title, but a certificate that conveyed co-ownership of the vehicle with the State. I was a cop and I wanted to know how this stuff really worked, so I began to dig. At first, I was only limited to NC Motor Vehicle Law books, but as I dug further, into other State and Federal Law books and their apparatus, and Badnarik was right. *The Manufacturers Certificate of Origin* (MCO), also know at the actual *Title,* is taken into possession by the State upon the purchase of a new vehicle, and in its place, a *Certificate of Title* (CT), is given to the new *owner* of the vehicle, with the name of the State and the new buyer information printed on the CT. What this does is surrender principal or absolute ownership and control of the vehicle and the rights attached, to the State. This allows *legal possession* of the vehicle by the purchaser, and thus converts those rights attached into *legal privileges.* This is the same process with boats, trailers, land, etc., depending on the jurisdiction and the property. Why? There are several reasons. One is because when the state is the principal owner of property, and the individual is the co-owner, or holds only legal possession of property, the state can then "legally" tax the property and control its use, as it wants to, by funding the implementation of secondary laws, or regulations. Also, and most importantly, such a scheme that transfers true ownership of property, or wealth, from the buyer to the state allows the state to avoid Constitutional restrictions that protect an individual's ownership of the property and their free use of it. This is where lots of "what if" scenarios and hypotheticals come into play, as it relates to articulating the need for such policy; "The founders didn't foresee cars." Right? Also, the fact that the State "owns" the roads is another reason for such a scheme. But recall, the "State" is just other people.

The question to ask now is, why is absolute ownership of property, like a vehicle, a bad thing? Because, this kind of liberty is not good for business and it is not good for "public safety." Being the principal owner of your property limits the power of the ruling class and of government officials who want to tax it for revenue to help fund local services, and, being the principal owner of the vehicle limits the power of government officials to regulate the use of the vehicle. Moreover, principal ownership hinders the *conveniences* of the state owning the vehicle. Think of all the corporate income that is secured through this kind of *co-ownership* policy, as it relates to property. Absolute ownership of property threatens crony-capitalism. True ownership of property empowers individuals and limits government. Again, this is not good for government as a "business," especially when the government can increase its own income tax revenue by securing another corporation's income by law. Insurance companies come to mind. Civil law, for instance, is in place to deal with accidents and mishaps between two parties, for the most part, as it relates to property. The "what if" scenarios made up by insurance lobbyists only rationalize the desire for their corporations to woo government into securing their income, and, thus minimizing the inconveniences of civil suits being the traditional discourse for dealing with property damage in response to accidents. Unfortunately, for government, such civil process would be too costly, thus the need to mandate insurance, which can be more reasonable if more options were unavailable. In addition, absolute ownership of basic property by non-government individuals does not secure a government's budget prospective, which then can shrink the workload of bureaucrats and law enforcement. Absolute property ownership also *forces* government to cut spending. Is this a bad thing? The forced taxing and registration of property has its history in governments, ultimately deriving from Monarchs, or Kings, who created the process to forcefully extract wealth from their subjects and then redistribute that wealth primarily among consorts and ultimately to fund the King's will and lifestyle. Recall

William the Conqueror. And, like the King's soldiers and Shire Reeves, who enforced such a scheme, the monopoly on force today in America mimics the same enforcement efforts.

Again, taxing and registering property, coupled with the forced redistribution of wealth, have a history in political philosophy and in past authoritarian governments. The founders, like Franklin and Jefferson, tried to establish a system of government that works against this history. The cops today enforce a modern legal system, which is specifically designed to work against the founders' effort to undo this authoritarian history. In addition, cops are socially engineered to secure this legal and *oligarchic* financial system through the breakdown of the separation of powers, training and legal updates.

Governments traditionally adopt and use various political and philosophical views as a means to create their own policies and systems of government. Russia uses the views of Karl Marx and Lenin, for example, while America uses, or used, the views of John Locke and Adam Smith. But it appears today that America wants more and more to rid itself of Lockean philosophy, for a more Market Leninist philosophy. Why? Because today, any property that has any value becomes a means to increase and sustain government revenue and power. Politicians today seek election on promises from the treasury, and once they are elected, their energy is spent trying to generate more revenue for themselves and government through special interests. The bubble will burst.

Again, I'm not arguing here for an abolishment of property taxes or the end of reasonable regulations. I'm simply trying to point out how it works today and why. A reasonable taxation on property, above the essential, helps to pay for local law enforcement. We all know this. Without this, residents would need to stay at home all the time, armed, protecting their property from criminals. Law enforcement patrols help free up people's ability to spend time away from their home, to work and travel. If the government's intent, however, were truly about securing individual liberty, the natural rights that are attached to the individual, and their general economic welfare, as it is charged to do, and as it swore to do, then not taxing property up to a certain value would be the most reasonable means to secure people from extreme poverty. This can help avoid the forced redistribution of *essentially basic* property. The Institute on Taxation and Economic Policy concluded in a study titled, *Who Pays: A Distributional Analysis of the Tax Systems in All Fifty States,* that the lower one's income, the higher their local tax burden, "Combining all state and local income, property, sales and excise taxes that Americans pay, the nationwide average effective state and local tax rates by income group are 10.9 percent for the poorest 20 percent of individuals and families, 9.4 percent for the middle 20 percent and 5.4 percent for the top 1 percent."[51.5]

Another example of the benefits of Allodial Title on real property would help limit the IRS from taking a lien out on newly purchased homes and land automatically, which it actually does, at closing, under the *Federal Reserve Act,* which plays heavily into the Tax Code, Title 26. The US Treasury itself has *first lien,* not necessarily the local Bank itself. This is because the property was purchased in Federal Reserve notes, or dollars, which has "debt labor" attached to each note. It's like being born and automatically owing money to the National Debt, which you do actually. The National Debt, in part, is actually made up of the interest that the government owes to the Federal Reserve for borrowing currency to help it function beyond what it takes in tax revenues, and your labor tax pays the interest. This Debt attaches to all newborn US persons. The income tax is a type of property tax on the labor you think you own.

This same kind of thing happens to real and private property. You gotta eat right? But, instead of absolute ownership, and like the Kings and many despots before, all property of value shall continually be taxed, especially labor, and for as long as there is a National Debt. In addition, and very importantly, owning property in allodium would not undo the lawful police powers the government has when crimes are committed against others. And, even if one did truly own their house, for example, allodium does not make one immune from reasonable search and seizure.

What can Americans do today to limit government intrusion into their private life and to avoid excessive taxation on their property? The simple answer to this question today is, sadly, don't own property. Avoiding the ownership of property today is the *new* and practical way to limit government intrusion. I write this as Jefferson and Madison role over in their graves.

Guns

We can all agree that gun safety and gun responsibility should be equivalent to gun ownership. Also, we can all pretty much agree that there are people who should not have access to firearms, the mentally ill that are easily prone to violence, for example. But at the same time, as it relates to the mentally ill, we don't want people in government determining who may be mentally ill, we want educated doctors doing that, absent any political bias. Once we allow people in government to determine who is mentally ill, simple political dissent will become a mental illness, over night. Neither can we infer that all mentally ill people are prone to violence any more than the non-mentally ill. Besides, there is no such thing as a perfect brain. So there is a necessary effort to find balance and common ground that, under our social compact, legitimately and lawfully prevents the wrong people from possessing guns. In addition, such an effort must not simply respect, but adhere to the 2nd Amendment, which is the Law of the Land. The issue needs to be approached philosophically and lawfully, not necessarily politically. Ethical dilemmas should never be approached from a political perspective.

Gun ownership and gun carrying, as the exercise of a fundamental, natural right, absent personal responsibility, is ludicrous and dangerous to other people. Thus, education and training, as it relates to such a right, and as a means to acquire and sustain such responsibility, is paramount and must become a collective effort. This section will not be a glorification of guns or gun culture. Such glorification tends to emphasize a lack of the education and responsibility associated with the right to keep and bear arms.

The fact is, a free individual is not truly free if the individual cannot, without government restraint, *a priori,* choose to be armed. Being armed makes the non-government individual equal to the armed government official. This is equality. Is the duty to carry a gun, as part of one's government job description, superior to a free person's fundamental right to carry a gun? Yes, if government is operating in Hobbesian or Blackstonian theory. No, if government is operating from a Lockean perspective. Thomas Jefferson said that, "No free man shall ever be debarred the use of arms."[52] Let's face it, there are many people in America who simply do not like guns, for whatever reason, and that's ok, people are free to not like guns. There are people who want to use government force to stop other people in mass from owning and carrying guns. This is *special interests* in action. There are also many people who do not like guns who get into government and then try to use their power to undermine gun ownership, which is unlawful and corrupt, because they swore an Oath to uphold the Second Amendment. The 2nd Amendment reads, "A well regulated militia, being necessary to the security of a free state, the right of the people to keep and bear arms, shall not be infringed." Notice the strong language, "shall not be infringed?" Black's Law Dictionary, 2nd edition, which in the late 18th, early 19th century, defines infringement as, "A breaking into; a trespass or encroachment upon; a violation of a law, regulation, contract, or right." *Encroachment* here is a strong word, used by the founders often. The same edition of Black's Law Dictionary defines *encroach* as, "To gain unlawfully upon the lands, property, or authority of another; as If one man presses upon the grounds of another too far." This changes the sentiment a bit doesn't it, from today's definitions of encroach and infringe? Trespass is a crime. Another good resource for understanding the terms of the period is the *Dictionary of the English language,* by Samuel Johnson, 1792. Here also the word *infringe* is defined as, "To violate; to break law or contract; to hinder." Now here is the odd thing about the word infringe today, as it is redefined in the modern Black's Law Dictionary, 8th Edition, for example. The term *infringe,* as in the context cited above, does not exist anymore. The term today, in the later editions of Black's Law Dictionary, is only defined in the context of intellectual property. Why is that? The word *Arms* literally means any object for defense carried in the hands.

The 2nd Amendment is the *Law of the Land,* and this Law was incorporated into the States as the Supreme Law of the State under the 14th Amendment, whereby State and local governments must also *obey* this Law. This was originally done to give the federal government authority over a State when the State violated a fundamental right. How has that been working out so far? Moreover, a gun is *property* first, principally when the gun has not been used as a weapon in a crime or by threat.

Gun violence is the primary argument used by many anti-gun people to make a case for gun control in the United States, and, gun violence is a reasonable argument. But there is a huge difference between gun violence and gun crime. Cops are lawfully charged to deal with gun crimes, which do entail some gun violence. But gun violence, by itself, absent crime, statistically entails self injuries, deaths, gun mishaps, accidental shootings, suicides, and the like, that are not necessarily linked to crimes. These are also not necessarily acts of violence. These statistics are taken out of context for reasons of manipulating the perspective on guns. As it relates to genuine or actual gun violence, which is equal to gun crimes, similarly, banning all medicines that can cause possible death, which accounts for far more deaths than guns, is also reasonable. The US Food and Drug Administration estimates that nearly 100,000 people die each year from adverse prescription drug reactions.[53] Where is the outrage? Gun related deaths and injuries don't even come close. In addition, according to the Center for Disease Control, nearly 61% of gun related deaths are suicide.[54] Where is the outrage? These suicide numbers are also then linked in as *gun violence,* which is purposely misleading. Neither statistical facts, nor all the founding father quotes in the world, are a match for anti-gun sentiment, however. The *gun violence* argument holds weak ground logically because the sound premises of *gun crimes* are not in conjunction with the unsound premises of non gun crimes, like injury and/or suicide, especially in light of the statistical deaths and injuries also related to gun shootings and mishaps by law enforcement and military personnel. The second leading cause of death amongst law enforcement officers is being shot with their own weapon. The first is heart disease. The latter premise of non gun crimes arguing itself into the context of gun violence as a whole, and as a way to establish gun control, is unsound. This is especially true in light of the constitutional charge that government officials not *infringe* on the right to own and carry arms. Going after someone who commits a gun crime is lawful and sound. Only one unsound premise, however, in the gun violence argument, weakens the whole argument itself. Moreover, in this case, the gun violence argument becomes another premise in an even bigger argument, gun control, which then, in the end, weakens the even bigger argument.

In political truth, the fundamental right to bear arms is simply a potential and theoretical threat to authoritarian government. In other words, people who are armed and not in government are a threat to the people who are armed and in government. This is classic *us vs. them.* These people in government, in all probability, hold an affinity, naturally or by conditioning, to the historical inequality of the common people not being armed, which has historically, in turn, allowed the authoritarian and brutal rule of dictatorships and despots. *Public safety* arguments are basically all that pro gun control people have, which is not argument enough to establish gun control measures in America. Such legislative efforts are silent *encroachments,* especially when the "legal" measures are aimed at the people in mass. Sound objectivity would infer that if guns are really bad, then cops should not carry them either. What does "shall not be infringed" mean? Jefferson said,

> "Laws that forbid the carrying of arms are laws of such a nature, that they disarm only those who are neither inclined nor determined to commit crimes. Such laws make things worse for the assaulted and better for the assailants; they serve rather to encourage than prevent homicides, for an unarmed man may be attacked with greater confidence than an armed one."[55]

In light of the increases in population, and the present day ownership of guns being more then there have ever been in America, gun violence as a whole, which encompasses gun crimes, is still the lowest it has ever been and it is still decreasing, according to FBI Crimes Statistics of 2012. This is why neo-progressives need to manipulate the statistics of gun crimes in with gun violence. In addition, in a recent study done by the Pew Research Center in May, 2013, it stated that gun homicides are down by forty-nine percent from 1993, which puts gun related violence back to the levels during the sixties, all in spite of more people having guns now then *ever* before. Also, the study concluded that such decrease in crime might be related to more people being armed, thus, "Despite national attention to the issue of firearm violence, most Americans are unaware that gun crime is lower today then it was two decades ago."[56] If the FBI, the CDC and think tank studies like Pew have all concluded that gun "violence" is down significantly, why the continual push for gun control? With record low crime rates today, why continue the push to militarize police? Even Chicago's new concealed carry law, which was ordered by a federal court that ruled the lack of such a policy was unconstitutional, has helped drop the city's gun crimes to a fifty year low in about a year. Law enforcement leaders in Chicago think differently, however. I wonder why? Gun violence, excluding gun crime, which includes accidental shootings, suicide, and the like, has been around since the beginning of gun existence. Only now is it common knowledge, because of media outlets reporting on the matters, generally by coercion, and in line with the neo-progressive effort to socially engineer people away from their inalienable right to personal defense with a weapon, and to undo the genuine equality between the armed government official and the armed non-government individual. Where are the media reports on the positive use of guns as self-defense? Even the Chief of the Detroit

Police Department said he believes drops in crime are because more people are arming themselves. Chief James Craig said that, "Criminals are getting the message that good Detroiters are armed and will use that weapon. I don't want to take away from the good work our investigators are doing, but I think part of the drop in crime, and robberies in particular, is because criminals are thinking twice that citizens could be armed."[57]

The accidental deaths and injuries from guns themselves, again, are not argument enough to undermine our Rule of Law or individual liberty. What is the difference in gun deaths and deaths associated with alcohol, for example, or by prescription drugs? All are heavily regulated already. The lawful difference is, primarily, there is no *codified* fundamental right that individuals take prescription drugs and/or drink alcohol, even though both of these lead to more violence and deaths in America today then guns ever have. This comparison seems a bit ridiculous because people are contemporarily conditioned that legal privileges are equal to inalienable rights. They are not equal. Drinking alcohol and taking prescription drugs are regulated, legal privileges. Being armed and carrying it is an inalienable right. All three sources of death are not the same. All death is the same, however. Therefore lets end the consumption of alcohol and medicines. Exactly, the latter is not superior to the former. A legal privilege and a right cannot lawfully be dealt with in the same manner, which is why this comparison is rather dim-witted.

The similar line of reasoning that compares the United States with other countries, as it relates to guns, is itself nonsensical because such comparisons tend to umbrella America and other countries into some *unionized* legislative scheme, which, intently I believe, subtlety weakens American sovereignty and America's identity. James Madison argued in Federalist 46 that,

> "Besides the advantage of being armed, which the Americans possess over the people of almost every other nation, the existence of subordinate Governments, to which the people are attached, and by which the militia officers are appointed, forms a barrier against the enterprises of ambition, more insurmountable than any which a simple Government of any form can admit of. Notwithstanding the military establishments in the several kingdoms of Europe, which are carried as far as the public resources will bear, the Governments are afraid to trust the people with arms."

Former President Obama praised Australia's very severe 1996 anti-gun *National Firearms Agreement;* "Couple of decades ago, Australia had a mass shooting, similar to Columbine or Newtown. And Australia just said, well, that's it, we're not doing, we're not seeing that again, and basically imposed very severe, tough gun laws, and they haven't had a mass shooting since. Our levels of gun violence are off the charts. There's no advanced, developed country that would put up with this."[58] This Act literally eviscerated gun rights. Even the library of Congress made note of Australia's Law as "successful" legislation,

> "In 1996, following the Port Arthur massacre, the federal government and the states and territories agreed to a

uniform approach to firearms regulation, including a ban on certain semiautomatic and self-loading rifles and shotguns, standard licensing and permit criteria, storage requirements and inspections, and greater restrictions on the sale of firearms and ammunition. Firearms license applicants would be required to take a safety course and show a "genuine reason" for owning a firearm, which could not include self-defense. The reasons for refusing a license would include "reliable evidence of a mental or physical condition which would render the applicant unsuitable for owning, possessing or using a firearm." A waiting period of twenty-eight days would apply to the issuing of both firearms licenses and permits to acquire each weapon."[59]

The government officials in Australia, as it relates to their severe gun ban, do not see their citizens as equal, but as subjects. America was designed to be a force against the history of authoritarian aristocracy, and an armed citizenry does just that, in addition to personal self-defense. Madison was clear in Federalist 46, "A government resting on the minority is an aristocracy, not a Republic, and could not be safe with a numerical and physical force against it, without a standing army, an enslaved press and a disarmed populace." America is still constitutionally a Republic. In comparison, Australian citizens rest upon the armed government officials, the minority. In America, the citizens rest upon the armed citizens, the majority, to secure liberty, thus corroborating Madison's point. Americans will not be subjects.

As a way to curb gun injuries and accidental deaths associated with guns, Constitutionally accountable States should, of sound intent, create incentives and motives for individuals to seek out more training and education on the responsibility attached to the right of gun ownership, maybe even a *tax credit* or a *write-off* of the costs associated with education expenses related to gun safety and gun storage, for example. Responsibility that is connected to the Right to Bear Arms, as with the responsibility connected to any fundamental right, or civil right for that matter, should be a primary objective within early public education, especially upon the charge of *just* government being created to protect those rights. Public education is government. Also, those who exercise sound responsibility associated with bearing arms, like taking courses on gun safety and who train regularly, thus acquiring a Carry Conceal license, should posses greater liberty within society, as it relates to bearing their arms. Thomas Jefferson, in a letter written to Giovanni Fabbroni, in June 8, 1778, in recognizing the importance of early edification coupled with the right to bear arms at a young age, was a primary factor in the victory of the Revolutionary War against Britain. He said, "I think that upon the whole it has been about one half the number lost by them, in some instances more, but in others less. This difference is ascribed to our superiority in taking aim when we fire; every soldier in our army having been intimate with his gun from his infancy." Technological innovations can also be a legitimate source for establishing greater gun safety. I personally like the idea of the smart gun. Unfortunately, this is also a technology that could, or would, be hugely exploited by people in government.

It is cognitively deficient that the idea of

despotism will never again happen in modern America, and therefore, the general people should not be armed. Again, have we evolved out of human nature enough where people can be confident that government officials will never again commit mass murders, democide, and/or force the arbitrary imprisonment of those who politically dissent? So history will never again repeat itself, because now we have trustworthy, smart and benevolent people in government who love and care for the well being of the masses above personal interests, and, such Laws as the Bill of Rights no longer carry force against the government officials, because humans are different now and technology makes the modern people and the Bill of Rights incompatible? Sounds stupid right? Like George Mason said, "To disarm the people is the most effectual way to enslave them."

The people in government who do not like guns, foolishly like to throw the *baby out with the bath water,* and it appears that this neo-progressive reasoning has become a matter of policy contrary to being armed as a matter of Law, for some time now. Rights that are non-threatening to government are the ones government seeks to secure and protect. But, when it comes to rights that may pose a threat, even theoretically, to others or to the people in government, then such rights should at least be reduced to *legal privileges,* which to do so would be criminal in and of itself. Our Rule of Law protects the minority from the majority, even if the sentiments of most Americans are to get rid of guns. This is also why, in part, the founders steered away from pure democracy and established America as a republic. Pure democracies can be easily subjugated to the whims of leaders and special interest groups, who then incite the people. Therefore, and this is why, in part, that the Reconstruction transforms the American form of government into a democracy, because now America can be easily subjugated to the whims of leaders and special interest groups. Campaigns on and legislation to edify people on gun safety and personal responsibility should be the response to non-crime gun violence and gun mishaps. The enforcement of Law, the Courts and jail time are the lawful responses to gun crimes. Yet this won't happen because keeping and bearing arms advocates the exercise of a fundamental right that the government sees as theoretically and potentially threatening.

Regardless of the numbers published to encourage gun control, whether by the FBI or the CDC, or whoever, the numbers are still not argument enough to undermine the Rule of Law, which is that Americans hold an individual, fundamental right to be armed, with a gun (Heller / *Palmer vs. DC)*. Sound, progressive efforts in our society are made when public policy regulations not only secure the well being, equal opportunity and the technological innovations of the collective, but equally secures and protects the fundamental rights of the individual. Such policy is not withstanding to the Constitution. Public policy and public safety are subservient to individual liberty and natural rights, not above them. The effort to progressively advance the common good is to equally advance the fundamental rights of the individual. To do the opposite is unlawful, yet these policies have become "legal," and such policies undermine the collective's well being. The collective is made up of individuals, who have individual rights and individual minds.

On the whole, what we have here, again, as it relates to our Constitution, are other individuals who hold to a different philosophical view of what American government should be, and how Americans should be, rather than what we have and who we are. Yet, the Constitution, and the Second Amendment specifically, is still the Law of the Land. And, even if the Constitution is scrapped and done away with, under a lawful Convention, the inalienable right to bear arms still stands and shall not be infringed. "Constitution be never construed to authorize Congress to infringe the just liberty of the press, or the rights of conscience; or to prevent the people of the United States, who are peaceable citizens, from keeping their own arms." said Samuel Adams. Oh but today the Constitution is *construed* to authorize government to do what it wants, especially as it relates to guns, which is private property first. A general example of this *construing* is the possession of a firearm by felon. Again, this is an area where the purposeful, over-complication of statutes, leading to hundreds of pages of legal jargon, is written as a way to rationalize, or interpret a way around the Second Amendment. In addition, many legislators who dislike guns attempt to elevate misdemeanors to felonies as a way to curb gun ownership even more. The right to bear arms shall exist whether government is charged to secure that right or not, as with free speech. American government is charged to secure that right, period.

Again, if most of the US population wanted to take guns away from the people who own them, the Law would prevent it because the Law is designed to protect the minority from the majority. Once more, the United States is a Constitutional Republic, not a *pure* Democracy. Article 4, Section 4 of the US Constitution reads, "The

United States shall guarantee to every State in this Union a Republican form of government...." This has nothing to do with political parties but has everything to do with a guaranteed *form* of government, which is the protection of individual rights against the will of the majority and Law Enforcement swears an Oath to do just that. Yet, neo-progressive thinkers try to thwart such an Oath through statutes, and/or public policy. Again, our Constitution is essentially designed, in response to the history of governments on this planet earth, to thwart negative human nature both in and out of government, and to equalize people in and out of government. The Second Amendment, therefore, makes equal the Law Enforcement Officer to the Citizen, as it relates to being armed. The 2nd Amendment should also protect gun owners from people in government who want to make mean looking and ugly guns illegal. Unfortunately, and again, scary hypotheticals and cosmetic arguments have been successful in legislation designed to ban many types of weapons today. It is unsound reasoning to argue that government officials are above and beyond reproach, when it comes to bearing arms. And, at the same time argue "service" and "protection" of the people's liberty. Liberty is defined, in part, by the fact that an individual can be armed. It is also unreasonable and unlawful for an officer to approach an individual exercising a fundamental right, like carrying a gun, equally to that of one exercising a privilege, like driving, unless there is reasonable suspicion, at minimum, that the gun has been used in a crime. Mere possession of a gun cannot reasonably be itself a crime, *a priori,* in light of possession being a fundamental right. Such reasoning is ludicrous and arbitrary. The US Constitution, again, on purpose, goes against the history of authoritarian governments and aristocracy. And, for a law enforcement officer to negatively respond to an individual exercising their right to keep and bear arms, to own and carry a gun in public, absent suspicion of a crime, as though the individual is exercising a legal privilege, the cop then, on purpose, sides with the history of authoritarian governments and goes against the Constitution.

Yet again, government is an entity, only made up of other people, who are no smarter or better than you and I. Until we as a species evolve enough, whereby the greed for money and power, authoritarian rule, the desire to control other people, the exploitation of the weak, and the use of violence to get what we want, are no more, then, and only then, have we no more need of a moral, codified force to restrict negative human nature within government. In fact, we probably wouldn't even need government anymore. This is what separates America from other countries in the world today, and what separates America from the governments in history. On the contrary, we humans have not evolved out of our natures. We must, therefore, for the time being, do our best to hold firm to the efforts our founders made to undermine the history of what governments have been like. Thus, public policy that is withstanding to our Constitution, today, only prevents us from truly progressing, and actually moves society backwards, towards the days of authoritarian regimes and the inequality of people in and out of government. The inconveniences of too much liberty are not argument enough to make policy whereby those inconveniences are weakened, for the sake of greater control over society, or for more convenience in exercising same. There will always and forever be stupid and morally corrupt people who seek to do harm to others and their property. Our Rule of Law is sound enough in dealing with genuine criminals.

Criminalizing any and all human activities and especially criminalizing the exercise of fundamental rights like bearing arms, and then enforcing such regulations by letter of the law only, will not fix the moral problems of society, but will only make them worse. On the House Floor in 1789, Rep. Elbridge Gerry of Massachusetts voiced this concern over the 2nd Amendment, "Whenever Governments mean to invade the rights and liberties of the people, they always attempt to destroy the militia, in order to raise an army upon their ruins."[60]

In addition, to address the arguments for gun control again, there underlies the controlled conflict of, "us vs. them," which is an ancient political ideology that has nothing to do with actual reality, but is creating political reality in America today. The *divide and conquer* perspective is doing very well so far, in socially engineering not only the people away from their rights, like possessing guns, but away from other people who think differently from those who do not like guns. Thus, the whole left/right paradigm, a form of mental slavery itself, has gained a foothold as a limited and narrow way of thinking, for most people, sadly so. The argument of our political reality being based in a left/right paradigm obviously has its source in this limited and narrow way of thinking, combined with restoring the subconscious historicity of authoritarianism.

Recently the District Attorney of Los Angeles refused to charge officers of the LAPD who shot over one hundred rounds into a vehicle carrying two unarmed women. Is this not gun violence? One woman, 71, was shot in the back. This decision not to charge the officers was a matter of policy and not a matter of Law, whereby the Commission *articulated* that officers were in fear of their lives. The car was not being used as a weapon. Thus, accountability is reciprocal of both people in government and people not in government, which is reflective of genuine equality. If the judicial branch, who also swears an oath, upheld the equality that the Constitution is intended to secure among those people in government with those people not in government, as it relates to gun violence and gun mishaps that cause death and/or injury, then District Attorneys, as a matter of Law and not of policy, would likewise charge law enforcement officers *equally* for the same "use" or "misuse" of a firearm, as they do with individuals who are not in government, and, DAs should even be more aggressive because officers are well trained and held accountable to the Constitution. Yet, the record shows that this is not the case, overwhelmingly. District Attorneys, for the most part, grossly abuse *qualified immunity* more often by refusing to charge cops who have "mishaps," or are overly aggressive with their weapons, like the firing of over 100 rounds because they were scared. These are character and educational issues that apply to all people. *Officer safety* is not paramount to the citizen's exercise of the right to carry a gun because such an argument would nullify the *honor* in swearing to uphold same, especially in light of the risk chosen by the officer. Where is the dignity and honor in law enforcement, if public policy prefers and enforces officer safety over the security of a citizen's fundamental rights? This is backwards logic that underscores the cop's carrying of a weapon, which is not a right, over the citizen, who clearly has the right to be armed above and beyond the officer's job description. Cops, in the modern sense, were created long after the right to bear arms was codified as the Law of the Land. Neo-progressive thinking will determine that this affirmation is ludicrous, and rightly so, when their reasoning is founded upon the unequal separation of the people in government with the people not in government. The latter reinforces the false notion that such actions are "heroic." A real hero, in my mind, was the Tank Man at Tiananmen Square.

Nobody here is suggesting a return to the Wild West. As a part of the social compact, reasonable firearm regulations are necessary to actually secure the right to bear arms, like the enforcement of private property owners not wanting guns around. Problems arise when regulations either ban or prevent most people from exercising the right to own or carry a gun, *a priori.* Again, the Second Amendment makes equal the citizen to the government official. Gun laws that restrict or criminalize simple possession absent just and adjudicated cause related to that individual, or simply because of a gun's cosmetic appearance, is not only plain stupid, but reveals the intent on which the people in government who create such legislation are limited in their thinking to their own political ideology, rather than the ideology they swore to uphold. For an officer to enforce such secondary laws designed to thwart the right to bear arms via cosmetic squabble, is more than likely an authoritarian in their nature and does not have the people's rights in mind, but rather his or her desire to control other people. Public safety is not argument enough to disarm an individual in public when the individual has posed no threat. There are valid secondary laws in place for such threats, like *going to the terror of the public.* In addition, simply responding to a call, whereby an individual has a gun is not argument enough to disarm an individual either. Absent even the mere reasonable suspicion of a crime, the seizure of an individual for exercising the right to bear arms becomes unreasonable and is against the Constitution. The gun is property first. Nor does answering a call qualify as reasonable suspicion or especially probable cause, and a competent officer knows this, no matter what policy may dictate. All the "what if" arguments and fear propaganda cannot get around this lawful fact. All are bad neo-progressive arguments and such arguments are only a means to *articulate* the disarmament of the individual, simply because of the theoretical threat, which only has an effect on those government officials who desire power over others and who do not see themselves as equal to those people not in government.

The Ninth Circuit Court of Appeals recently struck down California's gun law in, *Peruta v. San Diego* (2014), which mandated that a citizen must prove good cause to police as to why they needed to carry a concealed weapon. The "good cause" clause in the statute is unlawful, the court ruled. Such a clause creates an *infringement* for most people. The court ruled the law is unconstitutional, stating that citizens had the right to carry handguns for lawful protection in public. *Palmer vs. DC* also ruled that banning the carrying of handguns in public, even by non- residents, was unconstitutional. These rulings are in conjunction with the US Supreme Court's *Heller vs. DC,* and *McDonald vs. Chicago,* in which both rulings asserted that when the lower courts interpreted the Second Amendment to be limited to militias only, they were incorrect, based upon the historical context of the Amendment's purpose, which is to equalize the force of the people to their government. Thus, the US Supreme Court, DC Federal District Court and the Ninth Circuit Court of Appeals have all concluded that the Second Amendment protects the right of the individual to be armed, with a gun, in the home *and* in public, which is what is meant by to keep (own) and bear (carry) arms. Yet, even after such rulings, people in government continue to thwart the right of people to be armed, even law enforcement. They should know better and focus on actual gun crimes, or crimes that use a gun. Citing statutes and ordinances, again, do not justify the interrogation and/or seizure of citizens and their weapons (property) absent probable cause or even reasonable suspicion that a crime has been committed, period. Such actions are unlawful and are only regurgitations of socially engineered fear propaganda, hypothetical scenarios, threats of force and the threat of being caged. Such threats are illegitimate and reflect negative human nature on the part of government, which the Constitution attempts to protect the people not in government from.

True story: suppose you are a gun owner who carries concealed, with your state's "permission." You want to drive three states away to visit family. As you pass through one of the states, you are pulled over and asked to exit the vehicle. The officer asks you "Where is the gun? You are a gun owner, correct?" But you decided to leave the gun at home, because you understand that some states and their minions are unlawfully hostile to the Second Amendment. You explain to the officer that you left your gun at home. The officer then proceeds to force you and your family out of the vehicle and calls for back-up. Other officers arrive and one has a K9. A search of you and your family take place. Then a search of your luggage and of your vehicle takes place, while you and your family sit on the side of the road, handcuffed (policy). One of the officers explains, while securing you and your family, that they have *probable cause* to search you, your family, your belongings and your vehicle because you hold a concealed carry permit in another state. Wow!! Right? How do they know this? Well because in most states that allow concealed carry, such information is attached to your drivers' license information and tags when pulled up on a cop's computer. The information shows you are a 'carry and conceal' gun owner. Nothing is found during the search and after two hours the cops let you go. What do you do? Most people would do nothing. What you should do is sue the cops and the agency for violation of your 2nd, 4th, 5th and 14th Amendment Rights, in Federal Court. You are not a subject, but a free individual. This was clearly *unreasonable* search and seizure. I would even go so far as false imprisonment. Owning and carrying a gun cannot lawfully be considered *probable cause* by itself, at all. Period. Unless there is a fundamental difference in what is legal and what is lawful. The irony of this fiasco is, this particular state's constitution specifically reads in its declaration of rights,

> "The Constitution of the United States, and the Laws made, or which shall be made, in pursuance thereof, and all Treaties made, or which shall be made, under the authority of the United States, are, and shall be the Supreme Law of the State; and the Judges of this State, and all the People of this State, are, and shall be bound thereby; anything in the Constitution or Law of this State to the contrary notwithstanding."

In other words, the 2nd Amendment is the supreme law of the state, and lawfully so. However, similar to *Peruta v. San Diego,* this state is a *may issue* state, which means that a free individual must show "good cause" as to why they want to exercise their fundamental right to bear arms, thus contradicting, by force, that the Constitution is the supreme law of the state. This *may issue* statute was also declared unconstitutional in federal court. The state's attorney general appealed the ruling and in March of 2013 the Fourth Circuit Court of Appeals overturned the District Court's ruling in *Woollard vs. Gallagher.* This particular state is Maryland. In my mind, this is a state that rationalizes inequality for the sake of public safety. True equality, again, in the historical and philosophical sense, not in a political sense, comes down to force. When force is not equal between a free individual and a government official, in a free country, then genuine inequality commences. Patrick Henry said, "Guard with jealous attention the public liberty. Suspect everyone who approaches that jewel. Unfortunately, nothing will preserve it but downright force. Whenever you give up that force, you are inevitably ruined."[60.5]

These cops clearly and *consciously* acted against the 2nd Amendment, which is the Supreme Law of the State, and clearly violated the fundamental rights of this family, who committed no crime. The cops' argument is that the Law is different in their state and that they were acting in accordance to their lawful power. No! This is highly unintelligent. These officers were acting on their training, not education. Ignorance is blissful when such ignorance is secured within *training* alone, absent actual knowledge that comes through mere education. Like I said before, a police state can only happen when each branch of government is complicit to the other. A lot of times, training secures injustice, and it is unlawful power. Recall *Concurrent Review.* This is another example of where law enforcement is exploited and then socially engineered by legislation designed to undermine fundamental rights through the regulation of privileges. Driving is a privilege. Bearing Arms and traveling are fundamental rights. In this case, the 2nd amendment became inferior to secondary law or statute, a possession crime, which is color of law. Thus the officers went against the Constitution.

First of all, and yet again, the 14th Amendment incorporates the Bill of Rights into the States whereby the Law of the Land supercedes State and local statutes. This means that in each State of the Union, the Bill of Rights is the highest Law in that State, next to the State's own Constitution. Second, absent a real crime, a gun is property first and the owner of the gun is also protected by the 4th and the 5th Amendments, which say that probable cause and due process must attach to the confiscation of property. Once a gun is unlawfully used as a weapon, then enforcement action against the individual being armed is lawful. Third, it is morally absurd and despotic to falsely imprison innocent people who are merely exercising their fundamental rights. Even before the Bill of Rights became the Supreme Law in the States, Thomas Jefferson said, "The Constitution of most of our states (and of the United States) assert that all power is inherent in the people; that they may exercise it by themselves; that it is their right and duty to be at all times armed."[61]

Neo-progressive legislators and their attorneys like to manipulate legal language and thus structure "what if" arguments as a way to prop-up secondary legislation, which then stifles fundamental rights. Then they train cops to enforce such intention. Secondary legislation is statute, or public policy designed to regulate privileges and is inferior to primary legislation, which is the 2nd Amendment, designed to secure a fundamental right. Why is this so hard to grasp? This does not take into account the lawful legislation designed to regulate in general, however. So, individuals in government who are in positions of power and who hold a view of government that differs from the founding principles, which are adopted from Locke, will create legislation to inconveniently regulate the fundamental rights of the people through mere public policy regulations. This is what gives birth to the monstrous *legal system,* also known as the Leviathan. The lawful taking of property from individuals, by government officials, is only just as punishment for a convicted crime that is directly connected to that property. The due process of law is the Law of the Land in America and again derives from the Magna Carte, "No freeman shall be taken, or imprisoned, or disseised, or outlawed, or exiled, or in any way harmed - nor will we go upon or send him - save by lawful judgment of his peers or by the Law of the Land."

If the cops in this actual case were constitutionally minded and conscious of their Oath to protect and secure the fundamental rights of the people, then such a road fiasco would not take place. In fact, the whole gun issue would not have come up at all during the stop. The whole experience would have been associated with the privilege of driving, whereby the officer had witnessed a driving violation, instead of the officer randomly running a tag to learn information on a driver and using that information as *reasonable suspicion* for the stop, then taking it further by violating the driver's right to unreasonable search and seizure for being suspected of exercising their right to bear arms, all because the tags were *out of state.* These actions are the direct result of the *neo-progressive exploitation of law enforcement* that comes through a cop's training. It is unreasonable to decrease the risks involved in law enforcement by creating policy that undermines the very reason such a profession is honorable. If the government exists for the preservation of property, then for an officer to take a driver's gun, absent a crime, is stealing, pure and simple. And, such an act is immoral and a violation of the proper role of government that is confined to the US Constitution.

The United States is saturated with this type of enforcement. There is no room here to cover the vast amount of court cases that make up violations of the 2nd Amendment by government officials. Again, the 2nd Amendment is the Law of the Land and is to be enforced equally as with other Amendments. Imagine if Law Enforcement, at all levels, enforced the Second Amendment, as it should do, equally as much as it enforces the Thirteenth or especially the Sixteenth Amendments. Why is this not the case? Because, the 2nd Amendment empowers the people. The 16th Amendment empowers the government. One case I will mention, below, however, should be understood well.

In the United States Supreme Court Case *Printz vs. United States,* 1997, the High Court ruled in favor of two Sheriffs who refused to enforce the federal government's *Brady Handgun Violence Prevention Act* in their Counties, saying they believed the Act was unconstitutional. Again, recall *Concurrent Review.* The Supreme Court agreed. Within the ruling opinion, the Court concluded, as it relates to States' Rights:

> "The great innovation of this design was that-our citizens would have two political capacities, one state and one federal, each protected from incursion by the other"...."a legal system unprecedented in form and design, establishing two orders of government, each with its own direct relationship, its own privity, its own set of mutual rights and obligations to the people who sustain it and are governed by it."

Then, quoting James Madison, the Court's Ruling continues, "The local or municipal authorities form distinct and independent portions of the supremacy, are no more subject, within their respective spheres, to the general authority than the general authority is subject to them, within its own sphere. - The Federalist Papers No. 39." The Court basically ruled that there are, in concert with the founders established Rule of Law, sovereignty in the States and that the States are not subject to the Federal Government, nor are local municipalities, in this case, Counties, except by way of those *delegated powers* in the Article 1, Section 8 of the Federal Constitution and its Bill of Rights. How is that for precedent? The Sheriffs in this case were doing exactly as they swore to do, be a lawful check and balance against the arbitrary Act of the federal government. This check against legislation by law enforcement also applies to state law. When an officer blindly enforces any and all laws on the books, the intended separation of powers blends into one. First of all, society cannot pay an officer enough money to enforce every law on the books. Thus, officer discretion, as it relates to enforcement, is imperative. Blind public policy enforcement is not an act of valor, but an unconscious subservience to exploitation. The most important thing to remember about the 2nd Amendment is that it equalizes force between the people and their government, securing genuine equality against the history of inequality. Moreover, the 2nd Amendment also protects the right for "arms" to consist of any weapon necessary, like a bat, a sword, and the like, that can be carried in one's hands.

Self-Ownership

It stands to reason that if you do not own your own life, your own body, you do not own the products of your life. If someone controls what you can and cannot put into your own body, within your own home, you do not own your self. Like I've stated before, and I will again many times later, the Constitution was established as a moral force, codified to restrain the negative aspects of human nature in government. Forgive my brevity, but there are people who have existed in history who never should have, and people who exist today that should not. Specifically, but who are not limited to, those people in the past who have enslaved, by way of violence, other human beings to exploit their existence for personal or collective gain. These people are a scar upon human evolution and are the furthest from the most divine aspects of human benevolence. And yes, enslavement of human beings still happens today, especially within the context of forced economic activity and debt labor.[62]

The most fundamental of all the inalienable rights, self-ownership, has become the most damaged and the most subjugated by those in and out of power, in all of human history. And we are all guilty in some way or another. I am not going to attempt to rectify the fact that our founders owned slaves and personally benefited from them. I want to show how the Constitution, as a moral force, was arguably a hope for the Framers to end slavery, and why it took so long to do so and the difficulties in ending it right away. Thus, I want to dive into slavery, quite briefly, as it is the most abhorrent aspect of American history because of its blatant violation of human rights. All laws that pertained to the protection of property rights, as it relates to another human being as property, were, are and forever will be null and void. It was pure violence that made the laws work for those who owned slaves. Quite frankly, the Constitutional protections of property do not hold weight when it comes to people being property, period. In fact, such laws are ludicrous, nonsensical and were not even laws at all.

When Frederick Douglas was no longer a slave, he discovered the spirit of self-ownership and the fruits of his own labor. He writes,

> "On my way down Union Street I saw a large pile of coal in the front of the house of Rev. Ephraim Peabody, the Unitarian minister. I went to the kitchen door and asked the privilege of bringing in and putting away this coal. "What will you charge?" said the lady. "I will leave it to you madam." "You may put it away," she said. I was not long in accomplishing the job, when the dear lady put into my hand *two silver half dollars.* To understand the emotion that swelled my heart as I clasped this money, realizing that I had no master who could take it from me – *that it was mine – that my hands were my own,* and could earn more of the precious coin – one must have been in some sense himself a slave."[63]

Slaves were property, property of their owners. Slavery was a violation of not only natural, moral law, but of one's natural rights, which, again, was self-ownership. James Madison makes reference to the idea that laws are null and void as protections of property rights when it comes to other people being property, that it is mere violence that sustains people as slaves and as property, not law,

> "We must deny the fact, that slaves are considered merely as property, and in no respect whatever as persons. The true state of the case is, that they partake of both these qualities: being considered by our laws, in some respects, as persons, and in other respects as property. In being compelled to labor, not for himself, but for a master; in being vendible by one master to another master; and in being subject at all times to be restrained in his liberty and chastised in his body, by the capricious will of another, the slave may appear to be degraded from the human rank, and classed with those irrational animals which fall under the legal denomination of property. In being protected, on the other hand, in his life and in his limbs, against the violence of all others, even the master of his labor and his liberty; and in being punishable himself for all violence committed against others, the slave is no less evidently regarded by the law as a member of the society, not as a part of the irrational creation; as a moral person, not as a mere article of property."[64]

Stephan Molyneux, a contemporary philosopher, who writes extensively on politics and ethics, put together a thorough synopsis on the history of slavery into what he called, *The Truth about Slavery.* I want to vastly trim his presentation down and paraphrase his research into the next page or so: Slavery has grossly been a common and accepted practice throughout all of human history by virtually every government, every religion and every country that has ever existed. Even the Bible conveys advise on keeping slaves. Slavery was generally a result of a family's debt, by selling a child into slavery, or by being captured, either in war or by slave traders. In fact, the term "slave" derives from the Eastern European term "slavs."[65] Plato in his Republic said that owning fifty or more slaves signified wealth. During the time of Christ, literally half of all the Roman population were slaves. And, significantly, more than half of all the arrivals to the new American colonies were actually white slaves. At the height of the slavery of blacks in America, only six percent of the South owned slaves and 1.4 percent of the North owned slaves. This ownership of slaves was comprised of the very wealthy. And, twenty-eight percent of free blacks owned black and white slaves. People who were not wealthy, generally hated slavery. Historically, the reason for there being a rise in black slaves in the Colonies was because of warring tribes in Africa. They would enslave others blacks during violent conflicts and then sell them to Europeans at the ports, and to Arabs inland. Black slaves were basically cheaper than European slaves because there were so many. During the years between 1530 and 1780, for example, North Africans, primarily Muslims, abducted and enslaved millions of Europeans, including many American colonists. Essentially, slavery was not a race issue, at first, but a state power and economic issue. And, because of the increase of black slaves in America, due to their cheap purchase by the wealthy in the Colonies, slavery evolved also into a race issue. Missionary explorer David Livingstone said that in slavery, "truly Satan has his seat."[66]

During the height of black slavery in America, in both the North and the South, the wealthy would lobby individuals in the government to author statutes, or secondary laws, that would establish forced *patrolling* in the streets by white males, to monitor blacks and to look for escaped slaves, thus resulting in a "legal" use of violence against blacks, including blacks who were free. These white "enforcers" received pay by either returning slaves to their masters, and/or by reselling them, which was more common. For many of these enforcers, the legal use of violence against blacks was pay enough. The use of violence was a matter of public policy, and not of Law, whereby local governments legalized the use of *necessary* violence as a means to *enforce* the statutes, which attracted and gratified the authoritarian spirit within many of the white men in these patrols. Basically patrolling the streets and monitoring blacks was a way for many authoritarian men to satisfy their desire to control other people and be violent towards others, thus feeding into their own racism, and racism in general. In addition, these men who were forced to *patrol* the streets were heavily exploited by the special interests of the wealthy that economically benefited from domestic slavery, which was, again, a blatant violation of the most fundamental of human, inalienable rights, self-ownership.[67] Two really great books to read for further in depth history on this subject is *Christian Slaves, Muslim Masters: White Slavery in the Mediterranean, the Barbary Coast and Italy, 1500-1800,* written by Robert Davis, a professor of History at Ohio State University. Another book is: *Race and Slavery in the Middle East: An Historical Enquiry,* written by Bernard Lewis, a professor of Near Eastern Studies at Princeton University. So now I ask the question, why did the Constitution not work to protect such a fundamental right like self- ownership?

The abominations of slavery and the rise of racism itself, for the most part, derive from the founding of America, which, ironically, sought to abolish slavery along side of establishing Independence. Thus, being allowed to carry on as it did, slavery scarred the country. Here James Madison, as President, makes reference to slavery being a violation of natural, moral law, which, ironically is also the underpinning of the Constitution,

> "American citizens are instrumental in carrying on a traffic in enslaved Africans, equally in violation of the laws of humanity and in defiance of those of their own country. The same just and benevolent motives which produced interdiction in force against this criminal conduct will doubtless be felt by Congress in devising further means of suppressing the evil."[68]

Slavery was not a result of the free market, but by those who were immoral and who held economic special interests, thus exploiting the use of force in government with their wealth. In fact, it was the people in government who were bought and paid for by these special interests who actually banned and made illegal the freeing of slaves as a way to sustain government revenue, as it related to domestic slavery. If these people in government who profited from slavery had allowed the increase of slaves buying their freedom and the manumission by owners, slavery may have naturally been abolished in shorter time, absent a civil war. Later, it was the sound progression through the Amendment process that ultimately undid slavery. *Sound* because the 13th Amendment enhanced and secured the liberty and fundamental right of self-ownership, individual autonomy, while also keeping government limited to its delegated powers.

During the Debates, James Madison infers that such an abolishment of slavery could happen, absent the postponement of the abolishment of the slave trade in 1808, which was twenty years in the future, and as a natural course, if it were not for particular state governments that economically benefited from the slave trade.

> "It were doubtless to be wished, that the power of prohibiting the importation of slaves had not been postponed until the year 1808, or rather that it had been suffered to have immediate operation. But it is not difficult to account, either for this restriction on the general government, or for the manner in which the whole clause is expressed. It ought to be considered as a great point gained in favor of humanity, that a period of twenty years may terminate forever, within these States, a traffic which has so long and so loudly upbraided the **barbarism of modern policy;** that within that period, it will receive a considerable discouragement from the federal government, and may be totally abolished, by a concurrence of the few States which continue the unnatural traffic, in the prohibitory example which has been given by so great a majority of the Union. Happy would it be for the unfortunate Africans, if an equal prospect lay before them of being redeemed from the oppressions of their European brethren!"[69] (bold added)

But the States did not terminate the practice; therefore the federal government rightly ended it. The founders did early on hold the consensus that the Rule of Law would eventually abolish slavery if all people were free and equal, as the Constitution intended. "It is much to be wished that slavery may be abolished. The honour of the States, as well as justice and humanity, in my opinion, loudly call upon them to emancipate these unhappy people. To contend for our own liberty, and to deny that blessing to others, involves an inconsistency not to be excused."[70] On that note, and very importantly, emancipation could not have taken place in the Colonies without first establishing Independence from the Monarchy. Benjamin Franklin emphasized this by asserting, that whenever the Colonies had attempted to end slavery under the Monarchy, the King had indeed thwarted those attempts,

> ". . . a disposition to abolish slavery prevails in North America, that many of Pennsylvanians have set their slaves at liberty, and that even the Virginia Assembly have petitioned the King for permission to make a law for preventing the importation of more into that colony. This request, however, will probably not be granted as their former laws of that kind have always been repealed."[71]

Such Independence of the Colonies, I believe, would have never been actualized if the Founders attempted to first abolish slavery under a King, whose kingdom benefited from slavery. Thomas Jefferson noted that,

"He [King George III] has waged cruel war against human nature itself, violating its most sacred rights of life and liberty in the persons of a distant people who never offended him, captivating and carrying them into slavery in another hemisphere or to incur miserable death in their transportation thither. . . . Determined to keep open a market where men should be bought and sold, he has prostituted his negative for suppressing every legislative attempt to prohibit or to restrain this execrable commerce [that is, he has opposed efforts to prohibit the slave trade]."[72]

John Quincy Adams argued that the Colonies were not initially responsible for slavery, that slavery in the Colonies was because of the King. The Colonies originally sought to end the practice, as cited above. Thus, it was of the utmost importance, before abolishing slavery, to first free the Colonies from the King by way of Independence,

"The inconsistency of the institution of domestic slavery with the principles of the Declaration of Independence was seen and lamented by all the southern patriots of the Revolution; by no one with deeper and more unalterable conviction than by the author of the Declaration himself [Jefferson]. No charge of insincerity or hypocrisy can be fairly laid to their charge. Never from their lips was heard one syllable of attempt to justify the institution of slavery. They universally considered it as a reproach fastened upon them by the unnatural step-mother country [Great Britain] and they saw that before the principles of the Declaration of Independence, slavery, in common with every other mode of oppression, was destined sooner or later to be banished from the earth. **Such was the undoubting conviction of Jefferson to his dying day.** In the Memoir of His Life, written at the age of seventy-seven, he gave to his countrymen the solemn and emphatic warning that the day was not distant when they must hear and adopt the general emancipation of their slaves."[73] (bold added)

John Quincy Adams notably argues that Jefferson himself, who had slaves, was not a hypocrite, that such a practice had been cultivated from the Monarchy. This no way justifies the fact, however. To put this into context today, imagine believing something is wrong and immoral, but doing it anyway, simply because it is so common a practice amongst your class of people. Wall Street tactics come to mind, or a city charging people for water.

Freedom from such a Monarchical government was primary before attempting to end slavery in the colonies. Once Independence happened, then, the abolishment of slavery would naturally follow, in time. "Every measure of prudence, therefore, ought to be assumed for the eventual total extirpation of slavery from the United States."[74] The point I want to drive here is that the founders, most of them, were against slavery from the beginning, but could do nothing about it in the Colonies while subject to the King. And, after Independence, slavery continued as the result of the King's cultivation and State Sovereignty. Thus, it was the attempt of the founders, among many of the Sovereign States to abolish the practice over time. In addition, if the Southern States, primarily, would have not continued the horrible violation of the most sacred of human inalienable rights, self-ownership, through its enforced cultivation by wealthy land owners and their minions in government, combined with federal and state laws to protect slaves as property, recall Blackstonian Theory, the Civil War may have never happened. The Federal Government had to do what it had to do to end the Southern States' violation of the most basic of human rights, self-ownership.

Following the Civil War, the federal government, during the Reconstruction, rightly took it upon itself to amend the constitution, thus increasing federal power in two ways. First, the 14th Amendment incorporates the Bill of Rights into the States as the supreme law of a State, so that the federal government may have just authority and jurisdiction over a State that violates an individual's *Bill of Rights*. During the 39th Congress, Senator Jacob Howard, who helped guide the 14th Amendment to passage, declared that, "the States could no longer infringe upon the liberties that the Bill of Rights had secured against the federal government. Henceforth, they must respect the 'personal rights guaranteed and secured by the first eight amendments.'"[75] Second, the 14th Amendment created a Federal or US Citizenship, primarily as a way to protect newly freed slaves from State abuse. "It is a singular fact," declared Wendell Phillips, as Congress deliberated, "that, unlike all other nations, this nation has yet a question as to what makes or constitutes a citizen."[75] As a result of the 14th Amendment becoming the Law of the Land, John Bingham stated that, "the powers of the States have been limited and the powers of Congress extended."[75] He also said, as it relates to the Amendment, that, "It takes from no State any right...but it imposes a limitation upon the States to correct their abuses of power."[76] Therefore, and from then on, if a particular state violates the fundamental rights of American Citizens, whose rights are secured in the Bill of Rights, as the southern states did within the context of slavery, the federal government can lawfully intercede by force. The 14th Amendment was well intended. However, as with most government legislation that is "well intended," such intention becomes exploited over time and deviates into something else. The 14th Amendment is now the source for the federal government to usurp and exploit States' rights as well as to regulate the individual's finances, relationships, education, travel, etc. After a bit of hindsight, maybe, in 1871, Edward Godkin wrote that, "The government must get out of the 'protective' business and the 'subsidy' business and the 'improvement' and 'development' business.... It cannot touch them without breeding corruption."[77]

Slavery can be roughly defined as the ownership and force of human production, whereby an individual human or group of humans is property of another human or group of humans, and the one or ones owned has no liberty to do as they please with their own body and their own life, nor with whatever it is they produce with their own labor. Freedom can also be defined as being absent the subjective and physical restraint on one's property, body and mind. Thus, the most fundamental ownership in your existence is yourself. If you do not absolutely own yourself, then you cannot possibly truly own anything else, ever. Absolute ownership must exist somewhere. Right? Otherwise, how are individuals told what they can and can't put into their own bodies? Government cannot be the absolute owner of an individual, because government is an entity, incapable of the ownership of anything. So it must mean that the individuals within the entity of government own the people not in government. They establish and enforce the absolute ownership of other individuals for themselves, collectively, utilizing a vast array of arguments designed to protect an individual from him or herself.

> "If the natural tendencies of mankind are so bad that it is not safe to permit people to be free, how is it that the tendencies of these organizers are always good? Do not the legislators and their appointed agents also belong to the human race? Or do they believe that they themselves are made of a finer clay than the rest of mankind?" – Frederick Bastiat, *The Law*

Once you accept the fact that government is made up of individuals who then call themselves government, the more it becomes clear that the people in government think they absolutely own other people, who may or may not be in government. All the people in government really have on their side is the monopoly of violence, no more. Violence is what allows government to get its way. To illustrate, resist an officer and threats of bodily harm on you are regurgitated. With violence on their side, the people in government can tell other people what they can and cannot put into their own bodies. What they can and can't do with their own property. What they can and can't do with their own life. What they can and can't do with their own labor. This is why equality through force is so important. So the question to ask is, who absolutely owns whom? Would there have been slavery if slaves were equally armed? Doesn't take much thought huh? Just because slavery of the body no longer exists, does not mean slavery of the mind does not exist. The arguments related to these simple questions are vast and extensive, and are generally neo-progressively answered, contrary to Locke's view of property, especially of self-ownership. "Every man has a property in his own person. This *nobody* has a right to, but himself."[78] The highest of all property ownership is your own self. Neo-progressives feel differently. So another question to ask yourself, "If someone can tell me what I can and cannot put in my own body, within my own home, do I own myself?" Locke would answer "no." Thomas Jefferson made the point, as it relates to people being owned by other people, "The mass of mankind has not been born with saddles on their backs, nor a favored few booted and spurred, ready to ride them legitimately..."[79] But have they not?

Self-ownership does not exist today. Has it ever really existed at all? Maybe, for a King. Slavery still exists of the mind, and of one's labor, which can be worse actually. Because, the threat of violence keeps the mind in servitude. This is evinced not only by the *forced* tax and control upon one's labor, but also by the *forced* tax and control upon the fruits of one's labor, their property. Slavery also exists today by way of socially engineering the masses into the left/right paradigm of the political landscape. Such mental slavery *divides and conquers* the population, as in ancient Rome. As it relates to law enforcement, the non-ownership of self is likewise evinced by the exploitation of the enforcement of the statutes that are designed to secure all the aforementioned, all as a matter of policy and not as a matter of Law, which in the end, secures the interests of the state, which in its very essence, has become contrary to the US Constitution.

Postbellum America, the time following the Civil War and its Reconstruction, was a time when many state and federal statutes came into existence, as a "legal" way to regulate and control newly freed blacks and their property. Many such statutes were designed out of fear of a black rebellion, or uprising, because of slavery. So to try and prevent this, and to control newly freed blacks who were now freely armed, for example, governments created marriage licenses, property zoning, gun permits, property registration and certain property taxes, and the like. People in government, white people specifically, did anything and everything legally feasible to establish ultimate power over anything and everything blacks did and owned. Over time, these statutes encompassed everyone. Most of these statutes today, however, are still only "directive" in nature, which are unenforceable.

135

Civil Asset Forfeiture

In the 16th century, King Charles VIII of France said that his soldiers do not invade other countries and engage in warfare because of their pay, or for moral reasons. They invade other countries and fight in wars because of the plunder, or booty, also know as property. Do you actually think that when a cop today takes property from an individual under civil forfeiture statutes, that such action is of moral or constitutional approbation? The fact is, just as in history, plunder is the sweet reward for fighting in a war. In the case of civil asset forfeiture, personal property like cash, cars, computers, homes, real-estate, and so on, is the sweet reward for fighting in the *War on Drugs.* In Tarrant County Texas alone, cops seized more than 3.5 million dollars in property from citizens. Of this amount, $845,000 went to county employees' salaries within the District Attorney's Office while only $53,000 went to various nonprofits. More than $426,000 went to law enforcement salaries.[80] On top of this, *equitable sharing* of seized property with the feds actually encourages local law enforcement to circumvent state law for the sake of enforcing federal law. This is blatant corruption of and abuse of the Supremacy Clause in the Constitution, all for the lust of plunder. In fact, in 2012, Columbia, Missouri Police Chief Ken Burton, was testifying before the city's Citizen Police Review Board, where he stated that civil asset forfeiture cash was "pennies from heaven," to help buy law enforcement "toys." Think about that.

The modern War on Drugs was created by an *imperial wanna be president* who was nearly impeached for vast corruption, but resigned quickly prior, and the War on Drugs reflects that corruption that encompasses a greed for power and money. Drug laws are shaped more by politics than by medical or social concerns. In fact, such drug prohibitions began within the context of political racism and the greed for power, whereby minority factions were to blame for the "injustices" of whites. Minorities were seen as an economic threat to the "white" status quo. To quickly illustrate, opium was first made illegal in the 19th century because the Chinese, it was believed, were taking white jobs away, and they legally smoked opium. Later during the early 20th Century cocaine was then made illegal because Blacks used cocaine and were taking the whites' jobs away. Then it was the Mexicans who were smoking marijuana and taking the whites' jobs away. In fact, it was Harry Anslinger, the head of the DEA from 1930-1962 who stated in *The Emperor Wears No Clothes: The Authoritative Historical Record of Cannabis and the Conspiracy Against Marijuana* (1994) by Jack Herer, Jeanie Cabarga, and Jeanie Herer, p. 29, that,

> "Most marijuana smokers are colored people, jazz musicians, and entertainers. Their satanic music is driven by marijuana, and marijuana smoking by white women makes them want to seek sexual relations with Negroes, entertainers, and others. It is a drug that causes insanity, criminality, and death — the most violence-causing drug in the history of mankind."

How rediculous right? We know this is rediculous because of basic scientific fact. Principally, these minorities moved into America to pursue their own happiness and brought their cultures and recreational activities with them. Their banding together and working hard to acquire wealth and property threatened white populations, and, such recreational substances were made illegal as a means to suppress those minorities, imprison them and advance the whites' economic standing as favorable. This doesn't take into account the demonizing of such substances through false propaganda coupled with securing re-elections.[80.5] How is that for securing equal opportunity? These socio-economic facts are still reflected upon within contemporary prison population statistics today.

Such statutes and tactics generally only attract the politically corruptible. Civil asset forfeiture is a modern "legal" means of specifically increasing the funding of a government agenda and/or the wealth of a law enforcement agency and all agencies involved, because basic tax revenue is unfit to acquire such desired wealth. In other words, civil asset forfeiture statutes validate the legal plundering of property, nullifying the chains of constitutional protections, because such restrictions are just too *difficult* to abide by when trying to get the "bad guy." Civil asset forfeiture varies from state to state. Generally, civil asset forfeiture, as intimated by the Justice Institute,

> "Civil forfeiture laws represent one of the most serious assaults on private property rights in the nation today. Under civil forfeiture, police and prosecutors can seize your car or other property, sell it and use the proceeds to fund agency budgets — all without so much as charging you with a crime. Unlike criminal forfeiture, where property is taken after its owner has been found guilty in a court of law, with

civil forfeiture, owners need not be charged with or convicted of a crime to lose homes, cars, cash or other property. Americans are supposed to be innocent until proven guilty, but civil forfeiture turns that principle on its head. With civil forfeiture, your property is guilty until you prove it innocent.'[81]

EndForieture.com elaborates on the history of Civil Forfeiture, in part, by articulating what it actually is,

"Civil forfeiture is a legal fiction that pretends to try inanimate objects for their involvement with criminal activity. Civil forfeiture actions are *in rem* proceedings, which means "against a thing." That is why civil forfeiture proceedings have bizarre titles, such as *United States v. $35,651.11 in U.S. Currency* or *State of Texas v. One 2004 Chevrolet Silverado*. Of course, cash, cars and homes do not break laws. The legal fiction arose out of the medieval idea of "deodand," which superstitiously held that objects acted independently to cause death."[82]

Another term for civil asset forfeiture is *policing for profit*. It was recently reported in the Wall Street Journal,[83] for example, that police departments in Colorado and Washington States have lost significant financial incentive to the legalization of marijuana. Primarily, because pot is legal now in those two states, the cops lose a lot of the power and legal access to plundering the people of property. This is where *equitable sharing* with the Feds comes in as a loophole. Double agents, agents sworn into local and federal jurisdiction, can simply enforce the Federal Statutes instead. Crime pays, especially when criminalizing human activity is designed to not only secure revenue, but to increase revenue. Imagine if the United States, like Portugal, decriminalized all drugs, which has been very successful by the way, in combating addiction and the criminal activity attached to addiction. We can only really and legitimately deal with one, reasonably, not both crime and addiction forcefully. If decriminalization happened in the US, civil asset forfeiture would either die, unlikely, or be purposely linked to other new crimes, simply because the plunder is too good to lose. Cops would have to go back to enforcing actual Law designed to secure liberties and property ownership. I'm not saying they don't do that now, but to lose such financial incentive and legal power over other people's property, kind of takes the *zing* out of being on the streets, especially for corruptible authoritarians who signed up for the *zing*. New gadgets like computers, guns, military gear, LED lights and so on, must now become more of a budget issue for local agencies within States that legalize pot, now and in the future. In addition, outside of Washington and Colorado, probable cause has been increasingly abused within civil asset forfeiture patrolling, as it relates to pot. For example, at a vehicle stop, if no evidence of a crime can be visible within the *lundgable area* of a vehicle, and no consent to search is given, it is very easy for a corrupt cop to say they smell marijuana, or an individual in the vehicle appears to look like someone they have a warrant on. Boom there's PC. Cops can now scan a vehicle with an x-ray device, or call in a K9 to do a "sniff." The idea that implements are designed to increase the natural senses of an officer, as a means to get inside a vehicle, is in and of itself usurpation of the Law, because the intent of such apparatus is to weaken the restriction of the Law on the officer who wants to look inside property without probable cause. How does the 4th amendment protect the individual's reasonable expectation of privacy if privacy is no longer reasonable, but subject to technology that extends the natural limitations of the officer as a means to specifically chip away at such privacy? Then, the government gets mad when people get innovative as a means to *outsmart* the cops. Reciprocity my friend. More importantly, equality. Again, as a matter of policy and not of law, hypothetical scenarios become the primary arguments for such usurpation. If such ideas like civil asset forfeiture are that good and moral for society, the manipulation and exploitation of violence, by way of the barrel of a gun, would not logically be the means to employ such good and moral ideas. Fortunately the courts are ruling more and more against civil asset forfeiture. In addition, no such case to date, involving civil asset forfeiture, in and of itself, has made its way to the Supreme Court, and for good reason. Like the Patriot Act, civil asset forfeiture would surely be ruled unconstitutional, if it went before the US Supreme Court, which is why policy is in place like plea-bargaining and deals to drop charges in exchange for entrapment schemes. These are made before such a case climbs that high in the courts.

United States vs. The Motel Caswell (2012), Russ Caswell and his wife spent their life savings to build a hotel as retirement income in Tewksbury, Massachusetts. The property is valued at around one million dollars. During the course of daily business, various drug dealers and such rented rooms with the intent to deal drugs, absent the knowledge of the Caswells. Following a number of convictions involving the hotel, the Tewksbury Police Department teamed up with the US Department of Justice to seize the hotel under civil asset forfeiture statutes. The plan was to sell the property and split the proceeds. The judge in the case ruled in favor of the Caswells, however, saying that Law Enforcement "grossly exaggerated the evidence and that the cops did not have the authority to forfeit the property." The DOJ *wisely* stated no appeals would take place. This is a victory against civil asset forfeiture, again. It is a very sad case indeed, that free people cannot travel the highways without worrying about their hard earned money and property being stolen by the government, who is supposed to protect their property from theft. The justice system is littered with cases of cops taking cash and other property from people simply because they articulate that they reasonably believe such cash and property will be or has been commissioned in a crime. More often than not, it is far less expensive to let the property go rather than hire an attorney to sue the agency, which is the only way victims of civil asset forfeiture can get their property back. Thus, successful litigation of the agency is the only way the property can be returned to the owner. People and primarily their property are essentially guilty unless they can prove their property innocent. It's intellectually ridiculous. Incompetent cops know this and exploit it, which only reinforces the legal plundering. I don't even have room here to go into the IRS's "legal" exploitation of Civil Asset Forfeiture, as it relates to people's property, which includes currency.

Let me share a story about a similar case I was involved in while a supervisor on patrol. This is not a civil asset forfeiture case, but one that involves taking property. First of all, I did not personally participate in civil asset forfeiture, and I never did, simply because, in part, my right of conscience would not allow me, no matter the kicking and screaming of superiors. I simply wouldn't do it. I was mistakenly perceived often as "not doing my job." In reality, I really was. There were a lot of things I would not do as an officer, that I could do. Anyway, one day I received a call to assist some state tax agents who had come down from the capital to take property from a home. The residents, I was told, had failed to pay state income tax. Following a brief few minutes of small talk, an agent handed me a sheet of paper that listed handwritten items on it, such as a large flat screen TV, a computer, some jewelry, DVD player, and so on. They asked if I would assist them in taking the property, listed on the paper, out of the house and transfer it to the Sheriff's office for later pick up. I said, "Sure, no problem. Let me see the seizure order." It was silent. They looked at me dazed for a moment and like I was crazy. They didn't have the order on them and appeared disturbed, because I would not take their word for it. So I left, without assisting them. Later that day I was called into the Lieutenant's office because the Department of Revenue had called to complain on me, and asked who do I think I am? They said the agents were very embarrassed and that I should not be an officer. I said "whatever, they should have had the order on them." I explained to the Lieutenant that I would not assist them in taking property out of the house without seeing the order, because for me, it would be breaking and entering, committing larceny, and I'd be in possession of stolen goods. The next day I was called back into the Lieutenant's office and he basically told me that I was correct in not assisting the tax agents because, if the home owner turned around and sued, I and the department would also be liable. I was pleased. Yet, not because I potentially avoided a lawsuit, but because to assist the agents on their word alone, to go into someone's home and literally take their personal property from them, without an order, in my mind anyway, was wrong and unlawful. For the record, I did learn later that an order was in place. My actions at the time, however, were sound and ethical.

Marriage

The questionable competency within government officials created Civil Asset Forfeiture as a means to circumvent the Law, as it specifically relates to people's property. Similarly, through the exploitation of the term *civil,* another way for people in government to acquire jurisdiction over personal property is *marriage.* The First Amendment reads in part, "Congress shall make no law respecting an establishment of religion...." Recall, the 14th Amendment incorporated the Bill of Rights into the States, whereby state and local governments are lawfully accountable to the Bill of Rights as the supreme law of the State. Fact: marriage is an establishment of religion. Marriage is a covenant between two people, and /or two families, who exchange vows within the context of their faith and cultural traditions. Government did not create marriage. There is no way around this, or is there? What authority does American government have, state or federal, over who can marry whom, and why? There is no authority. In America, government officials must reinterpret marriage as a *civil or domestic union.* This way, in opposition to common law marriage, for example, government can establish itself as a third party within the union, thus giving itself jurisdiction *over* the relationship, via contract, or the marriage license. Otherwise, why would government even need to be involved in people's committed sexual relationships? The answer is, their property. This usurped power gives the government jurisdiction over all the fruits of the marriage, including children. Have a baby naturally, without a hospital or government involvement. Watch what happens.

The marriage license is a contract between a

couple and the government that derives from *miscegenation.* In the mid 19th century, following the Civil War, when interracial couples wanted to marry, they had to get permission and pay for it, as a means to be accepted by society. This also gave jurisdiction of the interracial couple's property to the government because such regulations had already been established for newly freed blacks. If one party of the union was black, then such regulations became justified. Black's Law Dictionary, 3rd Edition, defines a marriage license as, "a license or permission granted by public authority to persons who intend to intermarry." Over time, this proved financially beneficial for government officials, thus the practice of paying a fee for permission to marry spread to all people over time, as did the jurisdiction over their property, like income. The federal government then passed into law in 1923 the *Uniform Marriage and Marriage License Act.* But, being that marriage is a religious institution, such regulation on sexual unions between two consenting adults was constitutionally questionable. In fact, the US Supreme Court ruled in *Meister v. Moore* (1877), which has not been reversed, that state statutes requiring permission to marry are, "as before remarked, the statutes are held merely directory; because marriage is a thing of common right..." *Directory* simply means a secondary law or statute that cannot be enforced. One good example of this is in August of 2014 in *Brown vs. Buhman,* also known as the *Sister Wives* case, the federal court struck down Utah's law against polygamy as unconstitutional. Thus the ruling asserted,

> IT IS HEREBY ORDERED, ADJUDGED, AND DECREED that Utah Code Ann. § 76-7-101 (2013) is facially unconstitutional in that the

> phrase "or cohabits with another person" is a violation of the Free Exercise Clause of the First Amendment to the United States Constitution and is without a rational basis under the Due Process Clause of the Fourteenth Amendment; to preserve the integrity of the Statute, as enacted by the Utah State Legislature, the Court hereby severs the phrase "or cohabits with another person" from Utah Code § 76-7-101(1)[84]

The government does not have the lawful authority to tell individuals whom they can and can't marry, nor whom they can and cannot consensually live and have sex with. Marriage is an establishment of religion, and is subject to 1st Amendment protections from government intrusion. Special interest groups, in this case, those special interests of a religious nature, in particular, who want to control behavior that they don't like, generally concoct these intrusions and then lobby legislators to officially establish these types of regulations, as they originally did, in part, over newly freed blacks. Such authority is usurped. To get around non-enforceable statutes, governments then like to deny access to certain benefits and the like, which is a way the government, in the end, forces couples into contracts. Just leave people alone, right?

There are many such statutes related to regulating rights, which are enforced, yet unlawful. So today, by secondary laws, all people need to pay for permission to marry through the exploitation of a "civil" marriage or union, on paper. The ceremony doesn't really matter. This is illegitimate because such a law requiring people to pay for permission to marry is respecting an establishment of religion. Common law marriage has been done away with by the legal system because under common law marriage, people who have lived together for so long were considered married anyway. The problem with this is, there is no contract in place giving government jurisdiction over the relationship and over their property. Thus, common law marriage has been eradicated in most states. In addition, common law marriage has not been financially beneficial to government. Civil marriage, or domestic unions, depending on the state, are mere legal mechanisms to get around the fact that government has no real authority over who can marry whom, unless they attach the word *civil* via contract. Such secondary laws that criminalize cohabitation or even sexual relations, for example, between consenting adults, are all the more examples of usurped authority. These are usurped, predominantly, because the language within the statutes themselves, distinctively the elements, make reference to such a statute being null and void within the confinements of marriage. This in and of itself is making law respecting an establishment of religion because it limits the sexual behavior to marriage itself, which government does not have the authority to do, in America. Many argue that such statutes are necessary especially within the context of plea-bargaining and within circumstances such as rape, or sexual assault. These can be reasonable to a degree. But is reasonableness actually reasonable when the Law of the Land says NO? This is another example of Blackstonian theory in action for government gain. Since the Constitution does not specifically restrict the government from involving itself within marriage by using the word *marriage,* the government can take it upon itself to regulate marriage. Again, marriage is an establishment of religion and the first amendment restricts laws related to same. Therefore, this leads to the need for government officials to create lots and lots of legal jargon to get around it. The people in government should simply leave people and their property alone. Government should also stay out of the religious institution of marriage and let people marry whom they want, and moreover, stay out of people's bedroom. In addition, people and/or interests groups should not lobby the government's monopoly on violence as a means to force other people who think differently about marriage, politics, or religion in general, to be forced to comply with their beliefs, especially if such beliefs are contrary to personal freedom. It's wrong.

The fact is this, that through the excessive manipulation of legal language, whereby terms such as *civil* are exploited to criminalize behavior anyway, and circumvent the Law, the government can now take and control property without you having even committed or having been convicted of a crime. And, the government can now tell you whom you can and can't marry or whom you can and can't have consensual, adult sex with. These pseudo-rationalized and "what if" scenarios that allows such circumventions of the Law are all aspects of the modern, new style of progression (neo-progressive) in the legal system, as it directly relates to property.

The legal system today is specifically designed to work against, and to protect itself from the Rule of Law. The founders created a path to individual security against poverty and government intrusion, for free people, through property rights, which included absolute ownership of the essentially basic. The Rule of Law protects and secures this ownership through very specific and fixed Laws, not statutes. Rights and liberty itself derive from property. The inconveniences of too much liberty, in contrast to the history of the world avoiding these inconveniences, are, on purpose, and progressively the design of the United States Constitution. However, the legal system today is *redesigned* to subtlety reverse this, and digress society back into history, by re-establishing and *enforcing* the intended conveniences of less liberty, which necessarily must happen first through property rights. Guns are property. A home and land is property. Your self is property. One's sexual relationship is property. Income and financial assets are property. The fruit of one's labor is property. The more American governance happens through the barrel of a gun, the more corrupt and desperate such efforts have to become to get around the Law. This is a sure sign that the legal system is failing, and it's just a matter of time before all hell breaks lose.

I can't help but fear that another civil war will happen in America. This has happened once before, obviously. The Civil War was the catalyst to transition our original republic into a democracy and our Rule of Law into a domineering Legal System. The question is, if and when another civil war happens, who will the victors be and what type of government will they set up? Will the victors establish socialism, communism, a dictatorship, another democracy? My hope would be that the victors restore our original constitutional republic, whereby individual liberty, fundamental rights and true property ownership are the paradigms of law and order.

So what can we do? To start, as it relates to property, we need to put people into State Legislatures that will construct Allodial Title programs, giving people Absolute Ownership of their essentially basic property, via an applications process. This would, of course, include caps on valuation and taxation, securing people in their homes and on their land, from extreme poverty and homelessness. The question now is, would such a Bill make it through a legislature, to be signed into law by that State's Governor, absent big corporate lobbyists and big money politicians manipulating it, via amendments, that ultimately undermine the spirit and letter of the Bill?

End Notes

[1] Michael Badnarik, *Good to be King*, 2004

[2] Murray Rothbard, *The Ethics of Liberty*, 1982

[3] James Madison, *Federalist Paper* essay #62, 1788

[4] Thomas Jefferson, Letter to William Jarvis, 1820

[5] Thomas Jefferson, "A View on the Rights of British America" (1774) in *The Portable Jefferson*, Merrill D. Peterson (editor), pp. 17- 18

[6] Stanley N. Katz, *Republicanism and the Law of Inheritance in the American Revolutionary Era*, 1977

[6.5] Thomas Jefferson in a letter to James Madison on *Equality* 1785

[7] John Adams, Letter to John Jebb,

[8] Thomas Jefferson, Letter to George Wythe, 1786

[9] 28 US Title Code 3002 (15), (A)

[10] http://oll.libertyfund.org/titles/808

[11] http://www.salon.com/2014/07/04/we_the_people_are_violent_and_filled_with_rage_a_nation_spinning_apart_on_its_independence_day/

[12] Thomas Jefferson to Isaac McPherson, 1813

[13] Thomas Jefferson: Batture at New Orleans, 1812

[14] Thomas Jefferson: Batture at New Orleans, 1812

[15] http://www.constitution.org/jm/17870416_wash.htm

[16] John Locke, *Second Treatise of Government*, Of Civil Government

[17] John Locke, *Second Treatise of Government*, Of the Extent of the Legislative Power

[18] Thomas West, *Vindicating the Founders*, chapter 2

[19] Thomas Jefferson, Letter to Joseph Milligan, April 6, 1816

[20] James Wilson, "On Property," in Works of James Wilson, Harvard University Press, ed. Robert McCloskey, vol. 2, pg. 719

[21] James Madison speech in the Virginia Constitutional Convention, 1830

[22] Thomas Jefferson to Edward Bancroft, 1788

[23] Locke, *The Second Treatise of Government*

[23.5] *Women and Taxes*, written by Edward J. McCaffery, 2002, via the National Center for Policy Analysis

[24] Thomas Hobbes, *Leviathan*, Of Those Things that Weaken or Tend to the Dissolution of a Commonwealth

[25] http://reason.com/archives/2014/03/27/probable-cause-warrants-and-the-nsa

[26] Terry vs. Ohio

[27] Federalist Paper 51

[28] Julian Waterman, Thomas Jefferson and Blackstone's Commentaries, 1933

[29] Thomas Jefferson, Letter to James Madison, 1826

[30] William W. Freehling, *Prelude to Civil War* 1966

[31] James Madison, "Charters," in *James Madison*, Hunt

[32] Timothy Sandefur, *Property Rights in 21st Century America*, 2006

[33] Timothy Sandefur, *Property Rights in 21st Century America*, 2006

[34] Billings vs. Hall, CA 1857

[35]
http://hosted.ap.org/dynamic/stories/E/EU_REL_VATICAN_UN?SITE=AP&SECTION=HOME&TEMPLATE=DEFAULT&CTIME=2014-05-09-06-31-28

[35.5]https://www.princeton.edu/%7Emgilens/Gilens%20homepage%20materials/Gilens%20and%20Page/Gilens%20and%20Page%202014-Testing%20Theories%203-7-14.pdf

[36] http://www.dailykos.com/story/2014/05/09/1298205/-Sanders-asks-Yellen-if-America-is-an-Oligarchy#

[37] http://www.dailykos.com/story/2014/05/09/1298205/-Sanders-asks-Yellen-if-America-is-an-Oligarchy#

[37.5] http://www.nytimes.com/2014/07/27/business/the-typical-household-now-worth-a-third-less.html?_r=0

[38] http://www.bls.gov/cex/

[39] Henry George, *Progress and Poverty: An Inquiry into the Cause of Industrial Depressions and of Increase of Want with Increase of Wealth: The Remedy*, 1879

[40] http://www.washingtonsblog.com/2014/06/neofeudal-neoliberal-arrangement-since-need.html

[41] http://www.nationaljournal.com/tech/here-s-how-nasa-thinks-society-will-collapse-20140318

[42] http://www.cnbc.com/id/101046937

[43] http://www.alternet.org/economy/joe-stiglitz-people-who-break-rules-have-raked-huge-profits-and-wealth-and-its-sickening-our

[44] http://www.economonitor.com/lrwray/2012/07/23/why-were-screwed/

[45] http://www.washingtonsblog.com/2008/09/what-time-is-it.html

[46] http://www.businessinsider.com/harry-dent-demographic-cliff-2013-12

[47] John Locke, *Second Treatise of Government,* Of the State of Nature

[47.5] nlchp.org/documents/No_Safe_Place

[48] Benjamin Franklin, *On the Price of Corn and Management of the Poor,* 1766

[49] Benjamin Franklin to Robert Morris, 1783

[50] Thomas Jefferson, Letter to James Madison on Equality 1785[50.5] Twenty Years of Congress, James G. Blaine, 1884, Vol. 1, page 185

[51] Speech, House of Representatives, during the debate "On the Memorial of the Relief Committee of Baltimore, for the Relief of St. Domingo Refugees"

[51.2] Behold A Pale Horse, by William Cooper, pg 43

[51.5] http://www.itep.org/whopays/executive_summary.php

[52] http://www.monticello.org/site/jefferson/no-freeman-shall-be-debarred-use-arms-quotation

[53] http://www.fda.gov/Drugs/DevelopmentApprovalProcess/DevelopmentResources/DrugInteractionsLabeling/ucm114848.htm

[54] National Vital Statistics Report 2010 – May, 2013

[55] Thomas Jefferson quoting criminologist Cesare Beccaria

[56] www.pewsocialtrends.org/files/2013/05/firearms_final_05-2013.pdf

[57] http://www.detroitnews.com/article/20140716/METRO01/307160034

[58] CNN06102014170829

[59] http://www.loc.gov/law/help/firearms-control/australia.php

[60]I Annals of Congress at 750, August 17, 1789

[60.5] J. Elliot's, "Debates in the Several State Conventions", 45, 2d ed. Philadelphia, 1836

[61] Thomas Jefferson in a letter to Major John Cartwright, 1824

[62] http://www.washingtonpost.com/blogs/worldviews/wp/2013/10/17/this-map-shows-where-the-worlds-30-million-slaves-live-there- are-60000-in-the-u-s/

[63] Frederick Douglass, *My Escape from Slavery*

[64] James Madison, Federalist Paper 54

[65] http://en.wikipedia.org/wiki/Slavs

[66] David Livingstone, *Expedition to the Zambesi and its Tributaries,* CH 10

[67] Synopsis from "Freedomain Radio," Stefan Molyneux, *The Truth about Slavery*

[68] James Madison, State of the Union, 1810

[69] James Madison, Federalist Paper No. 42

[70] John Jay, letter to R. Lushington, March 15, 1786

[71] Benjamin Franklin in a 1773 letter to Dean Woodward

[72] Thomas Jefferson, The Writings of Thomas Jefferson, Albert Ellery Bergh, editor (Washington, D. C.: Thomas Jefferson Memorial Association, 1903), Vol. I, p. 34.

[73] John Quincy Adams, *The Crime of Slavery*

[74] John Adams, letter to Robert Evans, June 8, 1819

[75] Reconstruction, America's Unfinished Revolution, Eric Foner, pg. 258-59

[75] Reconstruction, America's Unfinished Revolution, Eric Foner, pg. 258-59

[75] Reconstruction, America's Unfinished Revolution, Eric Foner, pg. 258-59

[76] Reconstruction, America's Unfinished Revolution, Eric Foner, pg. 258-59

[77] Reconstruction, America's Unfinished Revolution, Eric Foner, pg. 489

[78] John Locke, *Second Treatise of Government*, Of Property

[79] Thomas Jefferson, Letter to Roger C. Weightman, 1826

[80] http://www.forbes.com/sites/instituteforjustice/2014/06/05/cops-in-texas-seize-millions-by-policing-for-profit/

[80.5] http://thedea.org/prohibhistory.html

[81] http://www.ij.org/policing-for-profit-the-abuse-of-civil-asset-forfeiture-4

[82] http://endforfeiture.com/what-is-forfeiture-more/

[83] http://online.wsj.com/news/article_email/SB10001424052702304753504579282940412941998- lMyQjAxMTA0MDEwMDExNDAyWj

[84] https://ecf.utd.uscourts.gov/cgi-bin/show_public_doc?211cv0652-78